96.72

0654

ed on ... fore

Jim Clark Remembered

Jim Clark Remembered

by Graham Gauld

Foreword by Jackie Stewart

PSL Patrick Stephens, Cambridge

First published — 1975

ISBN 0 85059 190 2

Filmset in 10 on 11pt Baskerville by
Blackfriars Press of Leicester. Printed on
115 gsm Fineblade Cartridge and bound by
The Garden City Press Ltd of Letchworth for
the publishers, Patrick Stephens Ltd, Bar Hill,
Cambridge, CB3 8EL.

Foreword

There can be no one better to write a book on Jim Clark than Graham
Gauld, for Graham knew Jim over the complete span of his great career. In
this book he has put the life and personality of Jim Clark across to the
reader in a more complete manner than has ever been done before.

So many books written on heroes have a hollow ring to them. Graham,
in avoiding this, has had the talent to stand off and look back from many
different angles to remember Jim. He knew him as one of 'the boys', as a
farmer, as a rising talent, as a superstar and as friend. This, in the life of
Jim Clark, was a rarity because he chose very few people to be 'with'. Some
of my early times spent with Jimmy were shared by Graham. In the dawn-
ing of my career I was hungry for information and guidance and Jim was
obviously the one from whom to seek help, but this was no easy matter. He
was suspicious of people, protective of his privacy, shy and to some extent
introverted. Once he established that I was not just a hanger-on he was
more than generous and gave me an enormous amount of assistance at a
time when I really needed it.

Later, when I 'arrived' in Formula One racing, we had wonderful times
together. John Whitmore lent us his apartment in Mayfair which we called
the Scottish Embassy, a small but cosy retreat from the hotel life I was just
beginning, and it was cheaper, something we both appreciated! What great
days we had: I finished second to Jimmy in three Grands Prix that year,
and for me there was not a pang of jealousy. He was the master and I, the
pupil, was proud to be second. 'We' beat everybody else. The chat on the
winner's rostrum would have made great copy for a Scottish nationalist
newspaper!

Jim out of a racing car, however, was a very different man. There was a
time when this enormous talent in a race car, this man who made himself
one with his Lotus, who made split-second decisions with almost extra-
sensory perception, made himself look like the proverbial duck out of
water. Such an elegant bird in the air, so graceful in the water, but just a
little ungainly on land!

Ironically in his last year he shed many of his previous idiosyncrasies; he
became a more confident public speaker, a more determined business man
and was more comfortable in public. Prior to this happening, we would
leave Balfour Place for a quick meal before going to a movie in London;
Jim would drive from one restaurant to another before choosing where to
eat. By the time we had gone through this palaver we had missed the start
of the film!

His life was not without complications. In matters of the heart he was
quite a wizard: Jim was not without girlfriends, the amazing thing was that
every one of them thought that she was the only one. But with Sally it was

different. Again he couldn't make a decision; was he going to bend on his very strong belief that a racing driver should not be married, or could he let her go?

Helen and I were both very fond of Jimmy, he was part of our lives. This book will help many people who perhaps never had the privilege of seeing or meeting Jim Clark to know more of his life, his family and his wonderful talent. Those of us who were allowed to share his 'time' should thank Graham Gauld for a fitting memory of Jim Clark.

Jackie Stewart
July 1975

Contents

Chapter 1 *Jim Clark's racing career*   9
Chapter 2 *Back home in Indiana*   58
Chapter 3 *Hockenheim*   74
Chapter 4 *What made him tick?*   89
Chapter 5 *The heart and the family*   102
Chapter 6 *Friends and admirers*   114
Appendix One   123
Appendix Two   127
Index   141

Acknowledgements

I am grateful to the various people who passed on illustrations for inclusion, to Mrs Helen Clark for the loan of pictures from her private collection, to my friend the late Jean Rischette who was a great Jim Clark fan, and to any photographer whose name I have omitted by mistake.

I would particularly like to thank the following:

Associated Newspapers Ltd, *Autocar,* Mr van Bever, Eric Bryce, Mrs Helen Clark, Michael Cooper, *Daily Mail,* Charles Dunn, Esso Petroleum Co Ltd, Mr Everett, Firestone Tyre and Rubber Co, Ford Motor Co Ltd, Geoffrey Goddard, Indianapolis Motor Speedway, Ulf von Malberg, John E. Milne, Olympia (Milan), Jos. Rheinhard, Jean Rischette, John Ross, Jerry Sloniger, Steve Smith, Patrick Stephens Ltd, Julius Weitmann and Gordon J. White.

Chapter 1

Jim Clark's racing career

Time has an anaesthetising effect on the memory. We can all recall an important date or incident in our lives, but few of us can place it in a wider perspective. To understand Jim Clark's career in its context we must remember that it spanned many years of post-war motor racing history: years which saw the twofold demise of the front-engined racing car, first in Europe and then, more dramatically, on the famous Indianapolis track.

During the period in which Clark raced, a whole generation of drivers disappeared, many as a result of tragic accidents, while the more fortunate ones retired. So, as Clark's career progressed, he found himself competing with a new breed of drivers whose outlook was different from that of the colourful characters who were racing when Clark first took to the track.

It is surprising to think that just one week before Jim Clark nervously took part in his first motor race he had been reading an *Autosport* report of the Belgian Grand Prix, won by Peter Collins in his Ferrari after the great Fangio retired his car. There were drivers in that race who are now just names in the record book: who, for instance, remembers the eager young Italian Cesare Perdisa driving for Maserati, or André Pilette whose son Teddy was to become one of Europe's finest Formula 5000 drivers in the 1970s?

However, on this windy June 16 in 1956, Jimmy's mind was far from the Belgian Grand Prix at Spa. He had problems of his own: he was about to race for the first time.

That he was destined to race was obvious to those friends of Clark who had either rallied with him or been his passenger in the dark-green Sunbeam Mark 3 saloon. The way he handled that car was sheer poetry and, though I

In the early days Clark's favourite Sunbeam Talbot Mark 3 was his only competition car, and he used it at driving test meetings such as here in an MG Car Club driving test meeting at Leith, near Edinburgh . . .

. . . and at local sprints run by the Berwick and District motor club on the disused airfield circuit at Winfield. Few drivers could compete with Clark when he drove this car, and he was a regular prize winner. Even at this early stage his stylish driving paid off.

later travelled with him in various racing cars on circuits, I always appreciated his extraordinary skill in that lowly Sunbeam. In it he had his hair-raising moments, such as the occasion he jumped a kerb on an Edinburgh ring road, proceeding down the pavement at high speed between a wall and a lamppost, and the time when he put the car into a field after a Young Farmers' Club party.

The week before Crimond he won his first big speed event — a sprint at Stobs Camp near Hawick — although the results do not reveal that his only opposition, an ancient Vauxhall, was a non-starter. To be fair, however, Clark's driving was brilliant, and he was beaten only by a Porsche 1600 driven by one of Scotland's best amateur drivers of the day, Peter Hughes.

Jim Clark went to Crimond ostensibly as mechanic to his farmer friend Ian Scott Watson, who had recently bought a remarkable DKW Sonderklasse saloon. This three-cylinder, two-stroke car had pretty good performance and, as Scott Watson was famous for his purchase of odd motor cars (he had formerly owned a Buckler sports car), it was no surprise when he turned up with this strange machine for a handicap event at the northern circuit.

I could never get attached to Crimond, as there was always a strong wind blowing across this bleak and barren airfield north of Peterhead, and there

This unlikely looking DKW Sonderklasse saloon was the first car raced by Jimmy Clark, and a few weeks later he used it in this Winfield Sprint. Students of motor racing safety will note that it was felt in Scotland at that time that you didn't need a crash helmet for sprints if you were in a saloon car.

were few buildings to provide shelter. Crimond is the most northerly motor racing circuit in Britain, and Clark's role at the meeting was that of friend and mentor to Scott Watson rather than mechanic — a part in which he was sadly miscast.

Once at the circuit Scott Watson put on his battered helmet and went out to practice for the handicap race. When he returned he had a brainwave and asked Jimmy if he would like to practise the car in the sports car race — you could enter saloons in sports car races in Scotland at that time. Jimmy agreed and slipped out on to the track; within a couple of laps he had improved Scott Watson's time to such an extent that a deputation from the handicappers bore down on the hapless Ian and informed him that he had been feather-footing in order to get a good handicap. Alas, Clark made it clear once and for all that in all their future sharing of cars there was going to be no doubt as to who would be the quicker.

Favourite for the saloon car race was Peter Gordon from Aberdeen in an Austin A90, but it was Pat Melville from Glasgow in a *traction-avant* Citroen who won the event and collected a case of Scotch for his efforts (we Scots presented realistic prizes in those days!). The race in which Jimmy competed, for sports cars up to 2,700 cc, was won by Brian Naylor in a Lotus-Maserati.

So ended Jim Clark's entire 1956 motor racing season. There followed various sprints in the DKW and his own Sunbeam, and his parents were pleased that he restricted his efforts to these events, as they didn't want to see him in motor racing proper.

The following June Clark again took to the track in the DKW and finished fourth at Charterhall in a handicap saloon car race. Things might have stayed at that basic level had not fate, in the shape of Scott Watson's insatiable appetite for motor cars, not intervened. On one of his trips to London Ian was offered a second-hand Porsche 1600 which had been owned by bandleader and former racing driver Billy Cotton. On impulse he bought the car, returned to Scotland with it, and entered it for Clark to drive in the Border Motor Racing Club handicap race, at Charterhall in October. Early in the afternoon Clark took a third and a second place with the car, and then he went out in the big event and won as he pleased. Two more successful races completed the 1957 season.

Looking back, we can perhaps appreciate what happened next in its true perspective. In 1958 you didn't just get the urge to race and then go out to find sponsorship. Apart from petrol, oil and tyre contracts — which came along when you were successful — there were few pickings for the amateur driver, and in Scotland at that time all the jam was going to one team and one

During the petrol crisis of 1957 brought about by the Suez war, Clark's friend Ian Scott Watson bought this Goggomobil economy car which featured a gearchange that operated across the gate, rather than fore and aft. Nevertheless, Jimmy Clark was successful with it in driving test meetings.

Above *Jimmy Clark's first big win in motor racing took place at Charterhall in Berwickshire when he drove Ian Scott Watson's Porsche 1600 Super for the first time. In this handicap race he won the Border Motor Racing Club Trophy, but for some people the lustre of victory was dulled by the fact that the handicapper was Ian Scott Watson himself. Clark's later performances, however, underlined the fact that he needed no help from handicappers.*

Below *At the end of 1957 Jim Clark bought his first sports car, this Triumph TR3 which was the show model at the Scottish Motor Show that year. He used it along with Scott Watson's Porsche 1600 Super for many successful outings, such as this sprint meeting at Stobs Camp, Hawick.*

The 1958 season with the Border Reivers D-type Jaguar put Jim Clark on the motor racing map. He always recalled his battles with their great rivals Ecurie Ecosse, and none were more stirring than those at the Charterhall circuit. In this picture Innes Ireland, driving the new Ecurie Ecosse Tojeiro-Jaguar, leads Clark in the white Border Reviers D-type with Ron Flockhart in the Ecurie Ecosse D-type Jaguar trailing in third place.

team only — Ecurie Ecosse. After all, they had won Le Mans in 1956 and again in 1957, and were at the height of their fame. The 1958 season, however, was to see some embarrassing new opposition from a re-formed Border team called Border Reivers. The Border Reivers of historical fame were a bunch of raiders who made periodic sorties into England, plundering as they went. With Jim Clark the Reivers were to ride again.

Scott Watson once more provided the touchstone to set off the spark of an idea. The original Reivers racing team had been started by a group of 500 cc Formula 2 and sports car drivers in the Borders, one of whom was Alec Calder, Jim Clark's brother-in-law and himself a brilliant driver in a TT Riley sports car. Now Scott Watson sought to bring the name back and persuaded Jock McBain and another farmer, Jimmy Somervail — who was himself a racing driver — to get hold of a good car and give Clark a real chance in racing. They decided to buy a second-hand D-type Jaguar which the Jaguar dealers Murkett Brothers had for sale, and which had been raced by Henry Taylor the previous season. The plan was that Jimmy Somervail, as the more experienced driver, would drive along with Clark; but as the season progressed Somervail realised that it was no contest and he eventually left all the racing to Clark.

So, after only five races, Clark was faced with a D-type Jaguar, and his first race with it was at Full Sutton. This airfield circuit was the Indianapolis of the North, and it looked like being a really quick one. The inaugural meeting was held on April 5 1958, and the racing car event over 500 cc saw Clark at the wheel of the white D-type with the drawing of a Border Reiver on his charger painted on the side. The event put Clark's name in British motor racing history books for the first of many times for, in winning one of the two events in which he competed, he became the first sports car driver to lap any postwar British circuit at over 100 mph. I remember him telling me excitedly how *quick* the car was, for he had never driven at much over 100 mph in his life before. As if this wasn't enough the intrepid Scott Watson announced that the team had received acceptance of their entry for the Spa 1,000 km race the following month.

If Full Sutton was quick Spa was frighteningly so, and I am convinced that

In the early days Jimmy not only drove the D-type Jaguar which was entered by Border Reivers, but also drove the van. Here he makes a fuel stop on the way to Crimond in Aberdeenshire with the team's Ford Thames.

this race, so early in his career, put Clark right off the Francorchamps circuit. To begin with, learning a road circuit was something new for him, and Spa was one of the fastest.

David Murray's Ecurie Ecosse team was also taking part in the event, and Jack Fairman took Clark round the circuit in a rented car to show him which way the corners went. In conversation afterwards Clark left no doubt that it was a numbing experience to be told by the jocular Fairman that he would have to go flat out round some of the long sweeping corners. Once out in the car he realised just how dangerous this was, and he couldn't get used to the wind swirls that catch you out at Spa, or to the difference in conditions at any given point from one lap to the next.

The deciding factor which consolidated Clark's deep-rooted dislike of the circuit was the tragic accident to Archie Scott Brown who crashed his Lister-Jaguar. Scott Brown, a fellow Scotsman who had lived in Cambridge for some years, was a remarkable character. He was a small man and, although he had only one fit hand, he used the two stubs which made up his other hand to grip the steering wheel. Although Scott Brown was a brilliant driver, on this occasion he hit the wet Stavelot corner when he didn't expect it and flew off the road. Clark told me that on the previous lap he had noticed a few spots of rain at the corner — Clark was running well behind Scott Brown at the time — and when he saw the pall of smoke on the next lap he knew that someone was in serious trouble. Clark finished eighth. He never forgot that race, and his aversion to the Spa circuit lasted for the rest of his days. Indeed, seven years later, after winning the Belgian Grand Prix for the fourth consecutive time, he despairingly remarked 'Why is it that I can never win at Monaco on a circuit I like, yet I win Spa four times on a circuit I hate?'

Back in Scotland he continued through the season with the D-type, the most interesting races for him being those against David Murray's Ecurie Ecosse team. Jimmy took a delight in beating Ecurie Ecosse and, though on the face of it this was pure fun, there was an underlying, more serious reason. Jimmy felt that Murray had consistently overlooked him and, in fact, Clark was only to drive for Ecurie Ecosse on one occasion — a year later in 1959. A similar thought was going through David Murray's mind, for he in turn felt that Jimmy should have approached him about a drive rather than

There were occasions at the beginning of his career when Jimmy Clark would show boyish exuberance. One such was a race at Charterhall where this sequence of three photographs was taken. Clark lost the car at the hairpin at the top end of the circuit, and spun into the infield. Annoyed at his mistake he accelerated hard with plenty of tyre smoke and shot away to win the race ahead of one of his great Scottish rivals, Tommy Dickson driving a Lotus 15. As Clark came into the pits after the race he gave his usual sign of approval.

Jim Clark's ability was first proved to Colin Chapman at this Boxing Day Brands Hatch meeting in 1958, when Clark in the unpainted Border Reivers Lotus Elite took the lead from both Colin Chapman (57) and Mike Costin (58), and only the intervention of a slower car allowed Chapman through to win.

link up with Border Reivers and become a direct rival. In truth both were wrong in their judgments, though David Murray didn't relish seeing his cars being led by young Clark in what seemed to be inferior equipment.

In August 1958 Clark and Scott Watson drove the latter's Porsche 1600 together in the 750 Motor Club Relay Race at Silverstone. It was here that Clark's driving first came to the notice of the national sporting press through Denis Jenkinson of *Motor Sport* who drove in the same team. Jenkinson was one of the first outside Scotland to truly recognise Clark's great ability as a driver. Alas, on this occasion Clark's team finished 22nd, one of his lowest ever placings.

Already, however, Border Reivers were thinking about the future and, since Formula 2 was a promising class of racing, Jock McBain and Scott Watson decided to have a look at the latest Lotus. This was the front-engined Lotus 12 which used the 1,475 cc Coventry-Climax FPF twin-cam engine and which was to emerge in 1958 with 2-litre and 2.2-litre versions of the same engine in Formula 1, with Graham Hill and Cliff Allison driving. At the same time Colin Chapman had the Lotus 14 (soon to be called the Lotus Elite) up his sleeve.

As Border Reivers had earlier raced a Lotus 11, McBain wanted to see Chapman and have a look at the new front-engined Formula 2 car as a possible mount for Clark. It was arranged that they visit Brands for a routine testing session where the team drivers and various other hopefuls would be present.

Clark was given the Elite prototype to try and liked it enormously; Chapman jokingly offered Clark a lap start in a ten lap 'race' in the Porsche against

By 1959 Border Reivers had bought a Lister-Jaguar and Clark began to race further afield. This car was very successful and was used for various events including the Bo'ness Hill Climb in Scotland, where Clark set a new hill record for sports cars. The symbol on the side of the car is that of Border Reivers and is an outline of a statue to a Border Reiver in the main square of Hawick.

Chapman in the Elite. Clark managed to winkle out of that one, as the Porsche was on road tyres. Then it was his turn to try the Formula 2 car. This was something new for Clark and he wasn't very impressed, even though he had lapped in competitive times on the unfamiliar circuit. When Graham Hill then lost a wheel and crashed heavily Clark's mind was made up — no one was going to persuade him into racing a car like that!

All was not lost, however, as Scott Watson's face had already assumed the wide-eyed luminescence of Toad of Toad Hall at the sight of the Elite. He agreed to buy the first production version for Clark to race and extracted a promise of delivery before the Boxing Day Brands Hatch meeting in December 1958, Scott Watson selling his Porsche to Clark who used it as his own private car. (That car, registration number UUL 442, is now owned by a proud garage man near Liverpool.) This Lotus Elite was the car in which Clark's real ability was impressed on Colin Chapman, for one mustn't forget that Chapman was no mean driver himself and at that time he was still a hard man to beat. As it happened, Chapman and his colleague Mike Costin had entered Elites for the Boxing Day meeting, and the thought of having five of them entered (Chris Barber, leader of a well-known 'trad' jazz band, and a US airman were also driving Elites) was probably an added incentive for getting the Scott Watson car ready in time. Nevertheless, it was touch and go, but Scott Watson and Clark picked it up on the day of the race, drove it to Brands, and started to practise. This was to be Clark's first ever race on the Kentish circuit, and in those days it was the short circuit.

If there was anything likely to make Clark boil inside it was someone else's assumption that he couldn't drive. He told me that he had overheard

Though lighter than the D-type Jaguar, the Lister proved to be hard work to drive as this picture shows. Clark drove it brilliantly in the wet at Aintree in this sports car race before the British Grand Prix. The surgery around the cockpit was necessary to allow Clark to drive the car in his straight-arm style.

Chapman and Costin working out which one of them would win, and that made him determined to beat them both. As it turned out there were only three cars that made a race of it and Clark, true to his word, gave Chapman and Costin one of the hardest races of their lives. They were running side by side round the circuit, and eventually Clark took the lead from Chapman and seemed assured of victory. Alas, one of the backmarkers driving a Sprite looked too long in his mirrors going up to Druids and spun right in front of Clark, hitting the nose of the Elite as he did so and taking Clark with him. By the time Clark had sorted out the mess Chapman was chuckling his way into the lead, and that's how they finished, with Clark in second place.

The Border Reivers were raring to go for the 1959 season. They had a driver of great potential and all he needed was a car. As the Formula 2 Lotus had been vetoed, they started to look round for something else. At that time big sports car racing was still in vogue, and Clark happened to like these often unmanageable cars. Listers appeared to be quicker than D-types, and one of the more successful cars was a squared-off version — unlike the Frank Costin streamliners which were to follow — which had been driven by Archie Scott Brown and Bruce Halford. It was advertised for sale and they decided to buy it. Clark picked it up from Luton and, despite a terribly cramped cockpit, drove it back to Scotland. Indeed, it always amazed Clark that Halford could drive the car as he was at least six feet tall, and Clark was only five feet six. Back in the Borders the rear of the bulkhead was removed and the seat pushed back into the space, but it wasn't a wonderful job, and the cockpit tended to look as though it had been opened up like a can of beans.

The Lister, however, was a potent weapon in Clark's hands and with it the Border Reivers went marauding on the Southern circuits. It was never raced abroad, and Clark used it just 26 times, although 14 of those produced wins. His best performance was at Goodwood when, despite his retirement after running out of fuel, he battled with his great rivals Ecurie Ecosse and led them.

David Murray, the Patron of Ecurie Ecosse, who never like to have his thunder stolen (particularly by another Scot), was upset that Clark should be racing in a rival team. In his turn, Clark felt that Murray was freezing him out. However, there was just the one time, later that year, when they got together at Goodwood for the TT.

This race had an important effect on Clark's attitude to racing, shattering a myth which had dogged him for a long time. The myth which was shattered — that of the unbeatable hero — can be found in the hearts of many young men on the way up in their sport. Heroes are made in the mind, and one such was Kansan Masten Gregory, in Clark's opinion one of the great drivers. Certainly, this boyish-looking competitor had wrestled with and triumphed over some of the most outrageously ill-handling motor cars in the course of his career, real 'beasts' such as Ferrari Mondials and Monzas. However, 1959 was a bad season for him, as he had already bent two of the Ecurie Ecosse cars, and on one occasion had been accused of leaving the scene of the crime by the simple expedient of jumping out of the car before the accident happened.

At Goodwood, Gregory was paired with young Clark in an interesting new sports car for Ecurie Ecosse — a Tojeiro-Jaguar. Designed by John Tojeiro, it had a long streamlined nose similar to the Costin Listers and was fitted with

Here, in a sports car race at Goodwood, Ron Flockhart in the Ecurie Ecosse Tojeiro-Jaguar. just leads from Clark, with John Baekhart in another Lister-Jaguar in third place. Clark drove brilliantly in this race and was leading when he ran out of petrol.

a very special engine. It was a Jaguar engine, of course, but Stan Sproat and Murray's chief mechanic Wilkie Wilkinson had decided to produce their own experimental 3-litre version. They used a 2.4 Jaguar block, bored it out and stroked it and, by using a special Laystall crank, they managed to get it to 86 mm × 86 mm, or 'square'. Then Murray approached Scottish motor cycle tuner Joe Potts, who designed and machined a cylinder head with the same layout as he had worked on for the late Bob McIntyre's Norton racing motorbikes. To finish it off, Stan Sproat set to and hand cut all the pistons to suit the head, using piston blanks and rubbings.

The race saw Clark lapping as fast as Gregory, and the joyful realisation came to Jimmy that he could beat his hero in the same car and on the same circuit. Just when it looked as though they were going to be well placed, Gregory arrived at Woodcote far too fast and continued straight over the road, ramming the banking head-first. I was an eye witness to this particular accident and, when the car hit the banking, Gregory shot from the cockpit like a pea out of a pod and flew about 15 feet into the air, clearing the whole banking and breaking his arm as he landed. Some time later I spoke to Ferrari driver Olivier Gendebien, who happened to be slightly ahead of Gregory going into the corner, and he remarked that he couldn't understand how Masten was going to manage to overtake him on the outside and, when he glanced across, he was amazed to see the American struggling to get up on to the seat of the car. Had he stayed in the car, Masten Gregory would not have become the diamond merchant he is today.

Another dramatic episode occurred in this race when Moss came into the

In the 1959 Boxing Day Brands Hatch meeting, Clark was back with another Border Reivers Lotus Elite, this time battling with Graham Warner's similar car (76) and Richard Shepherd Barron's Alfa Romeo. In this event Clark drove with great brio, but the car lost a wheel and he retired.

pits with his leading 3-litre Aston Martin DBR1. While being refuelled the car caught fire, setting light to the wooden pit counter. Little did Clark know, as he watched the event, that he would be driving the self-same car in the near future.

Throughout the 1959 season Clark had also driven the Lotus Elite successfully in the *Autosport* World Cup races, and he took part in his first Le Mans race.

I could never work out whether he liked Le Mans or not. He certainly felt that there were too many 'rabbits' out on the track, and didn't like the look or the driving styles of some of the second drivers, but then nearly every major driver at one time or another has shared this opinion. At times Clark said he enjoyed it and at others he said he hated it but, whatever the case, he finished with the race completely when the organisers refused to let Colin Chapman race the Lotus 23, and he vowed never to compete there again. Quite recently Colin Chapman told me that he had tried in vain to change Jimmy's mind about Le Mans.

Back in 1959 there was a touch of Fred Carno about the Le Mans entry. Scott Watson, bold as brass, had entered his white car, but Lotus hadn't had time to prepare it so Reivers withdrew the car. Then Chapman felt he would like to keep the entry and offered Reivers another car on condition that they drive under Team Lotus, but they refused and eventually they were lent a works car and ran it under the Border Reivers banner. The only concession to Lotus was that, instead of having Scotsman Tommy Dickson as his co-driver, Clark raced with a young English driver from the squirearchy called John Whitmore. John, later to become Sir John Whitmore, became a great friend of Clark, and in that same season he borrowed the Border Reivers Lister for a race at Charterhall. That year Aston Martin finished first and second at Le Mans, with Clark and Whitmore tenth overall, despite a total of two and a half hours in pit stops which cost them three places.

Jimmy Clark at Bo'ness again, this time in the Lotus Elite with which he won his class and set a new record. The Bo'ness hill climb course no longer exists since a housing estate has been built across the upper reaches.

At the 1959 Tourist Trophy Race at Goodwood the works Aston Martin DBR1 3000 caught fire and was burned out at the pits, but for the 1960 season Border Reivers bought the car after it had been rebuilt, and it was used successfully that year, particularly at Le Mans. In this picture Jimmy Clark is seen well on his way to yet another win at Charterhall driving this car. The odd shape at the rear is due to a ruling that year about luggage space in sports cars.

By now Clark's performances were getting him recognition in the motoring press and, whereas he was closer to Colin Chapman after his Elite successes, it was actually Reg Parnell, one of Britain's best racing drivers of the immediate post-war period, who really saw the potential in this young man. This is not so surprising when you realise that Reg, God rest his soul, was being given a blow-by-blow description of Clark's career by Jock McBain, the man behind Border Reivers and a contemporary of Parnell. One can imagine the ebullient Jock telling Parnell all about the team's young prodigy, and so it was that Clark was invited to have a trial in a couple of Aston Martin sports cars at Goodwood. As usual, Clark was wary. He knew that Parnell was going to be needing drivers for the Formula 1 Grand Prix Aston Martin and, although the idea of driving a Grand Prix car fascinated him, he didn't feel that he was ready yet. Also he was worried about how he would meet his responsibilities on the farm if he agreed to race more regularly.

It was late January 1960 and, at about the same time, thousands of miles away in the Argentine, Innes Ireland was racing the rear-engined Lotus 18 Grand Prix car for the first time.

Back home the trial at Goodwood proved to be very successful and had two direct results. First, Clark was signed to drive the Aston Martin Grand Prix car along with Roy Salvadori, the team leader, and second, Jock McBain did a deal to buy the rebuilt hulk of the Aston Martin DBR1 which had been burned out at the TT.

On that same day, Clark was able to drive the Formula Junior Lotus for, by what seemed a strange coincidence, Mike Costin happened to be there testing. Parnell agreed that Jimmy should try the car, and Clark was impressed by the handling. Little did Parnell know that it was Clark who had tipped off Colin Chapman about the Aston Martin test, so there was really no coincidence at all.

Clark, therefore, was faced with two people trying to sign him up at the same time. He chose Aston Martin for Formula 1 — probably with Jock McBain's prompting — and signed for Lotus to drive Formula Junior and Formula 2.

Unfortunately, he never drove an Aston Martin in a race, for the company appeared to have burned their fingers on the Formula 1 effort and, though a new independent rear suspension model was produced in time for the British Grand Prix, the whole effort was running at half-strength. They missed the Argentine race and Monaco (where Salvadori drove a Cooper) and sent only one car to Zandvoort for the Dutch Grand Prix, and even that was subsequently withdrawn. Meanwhile, Colin Chapman had lost John Surtees for the race due to a clash with a motor cycle meeting, and so had a spare Formula 1 car which he offered to Clark. At this stage Clark's future in Grand Prix racing was secure, for he had been offered a full contract with Lotus should anything happen to Aston Martin, and from that Zandvoort race onwards Clark was to drive almost exclusively for Lotus.

Much to Clark's — and everyone else's surprise, when it came to the race he found himself battling for fourth place with Graham Hill's BRM; but it was a short-lived success, as the gearbox began to seize up and he retired in the 43rd lap.

Two weeks later he was back in a Formula 1 Lotus at the Belgian Grand

By 1959 Jimmy Clark was a familiar figure in North of England events and here, at the Mallory Park circuit in September of that year, he leads a sports car race from Malcolm Wayne's Elva Courier.

Above *Even in 1960 Jimmy Clark was still wearing his original crash helmet and his familiar tinted air-force goggles. Here he gives his usual acknowledgement to the author on another victory.*

Opposite *Clark in 1960 about to set off at Goodwood with the Formula Junior Lotus.*

Prix. The memory of Archie Scott Brown's death at Spa was still alive, and in this race two more drivers were to be killed, including Clark's team-mate Alan Stacey in another Lotus. Altogether it was a tragic and worrying weekend. It started in practice with Alan Stacey breaking a bolt in his steering, then Stirling Moss (also driving a Lotus) had a rear stub axle break at over 130 mph. Moss was thrown out of the car and both his legs were broken. Then the steering column of Michael Taylor's Lotus also broke and he too crashed heavily.

In the race Clark's car wasn't running properly and he had to call into the pits to have the carburettors checked. When he went out again he was one of the first drivers on the scene of Chris Bristow's tragic accident in his Cooper. Bristow was a determined and forceful young driver with a promising career in racing, but on this occasion he tried to overtake the Belgian 'hotshoe' Willy Mairesse on the outside of the Burneville bend, and failed. The car went out of control and Bristow was thrown out and killed. Although he didn't see the accident, Clark saw the marshals taking Bristow's body off the track and he was horrified. After the race his horror was compounded when he heard that his team-mate Alan Stacey had been killed after a pheasant flew into his face. From then on Clark had a fear of birds, and it is ironic that some years later he too was hit in the face by a bird at Rheims, but suffered nothing worse than severe bruising and a black eye.

Throughout that year Clark proved his skill not only in Grand Prix races but also in Formula Junior. (The modern equivalent of this might be to have James Hunt running in Formula 1 and Formula Ford at the same time.) Interspersed between these races were Formula 2 events for Lotus and a few

Top *The only occasion on which Jimmy Clark drove a single-seater racing car in Scotland was at Charterhall in 1960, when he brought the factory Lotus 18 Junior to race in a Formula Libre event. As can be seen it was very much a Libre event, Clark coming up to pass a TVR on a hairpin. Jimmy wanted to race back in Scotland later in his career, but his schedule after 1960 was such that it never happened, save for the occasional drive in a sports car.*

Above *At Le Mans in 1960 Jimmy Clark shared the Aston Martin with Roy Salvadori, the pair finishing third overall and winning the Motor Trophy. They were presented with the trophy in Berwick, and the car was photographed at Berwick harbour. The small light inset in the grille of the car is a signalling light for Le Mans.*

events in the Border Reivers Aston Martin DBR1. The most important of these Reivers races was Le Mans. Aston Martin had withdrawn their factory team from sports car racing, so that any Aston Martin threat to the Ferraris had to come from private owners. The Reivers entered their car for Clark to drive, but in the end the team was managed by Reg Parnell, and Parnell arranged for Roy Salvadori to be Clark's co-driver. As usual, Clark was in good form and first away at the start, and he and Salvadori were able to take third place at the end of the 24 hours, 100 miles behind the winning Ferrari driven by Paul Frère and Olivier Gendebien.

The 1960 season had been a hectic one for Clark, during which not only had he visited the United States, but also he had driven the Lotus 18 in some of the Tasman races in Australia and New Zealand.

Towards the end of the season Clark was approached by a number of teams, including Ferrari and Porsche, to sign Formula 1 contracts, but he had a close rapport with Colin Chapman which was to grow and be enriched as each season went by, and he was not tempted to stray. In return, Chapman lavished all of his attention on his prodigy, occasionally, it seemed, to the detriment of other drivers in the team.

In 1961 Lotus introduced the Lotus 21 in time for the Monaco Grand Prix, to conform with the change in Formula 1 regulations. This change reduced the maximum engine capacity of Grand Prix cars from 2½ to 1½ litres, much to the manufacturers' consternation. While most of the British were arguing about it, Ferrari had been developing his own 1½-litre engine which was to dominate this season, giving Phil Hill the World Championship. The new Formula brought Porsche more into the running, but they raced for the whole 1961 season with their four-cylinder engines, since the flat-eight had not been fully developed.

The Lotus 21 was very similar to the Lotus 18 of the previous year, but it had a much smoother, cigar-shaped body. The engine was the Coventry-Climax FPF which had been produced in various capacity forms by juggling the bore and stroke around. This Mark 2 engine, as it was called, had a shortened stroke, giving it a capacity of 1,475 cc, and it produced 152 bhp.

Throughout the year the Lotuses had to slipstream like mad whenever the Ferraris were around for, with more than 190 bhp being produced by the new Ferrari V6 engine, the Lotuses could not be competitive in straight-line motoring. If nothing else, the season made Clark really fight for his money, and he seemed to revel in being the green meat in the crimson Ferrari sandwich.

At Monaco Clark was third fastest on the grid to Moss' older Lotus and Richie Ginther's Ferrari. Later, in practice, Clark wiped the car up against a guard-rail and the mechanics had to work hard to repair it in time. On top of this Innes Ireland had shunted the other Lotus impressively in the tunnel and was taken to hospital. Lotus' luck was out, it seemed, for in the race Clark's ignition lead came loose and he finished at the back of the field after a pit stop.

In the Dutch Grand Prix, however, Clark proved to be a real thorn in the flesh of the Ferrari team, harrying von Trips and Ginther all the way. Looking back now at the cars in that race, and bearing in mind present-day views about aerodynamics, it can be seen that one of the main reasons for Clark's success that season was the body design of the Lotus 21. Compared to the Lotus 18 it had a much smaller frontal area, even smaller than the successful Ferraris. That year the Ferraris were using the 'nostril' nose cones which, although decorative, were not very effective because the radiator provided quite a large and exposed piece of frontal area. That Dutch race also saw another milestone in racing for, in winning his first Grand Prix race, von Trips also made it the first Grand Prix victory by a German driver since 1939.

From Monaco it was back to Spa, where the extra power of the Ferraris was just too much for the opposition, and this time only John Surtees in his Cooper could get among them in practice. Clark had a new car for the race, but he wasn't very happy with it. Added to this, Cliff Allison had crashed his UDT-Lotus heavily — an accident which finished his racing career — so once more the spectre of Spa was hanging over Jimmy. For once he didn't tiger the car as he knew the odds were stacked against victory, and he finished second to last, six laps behind the leader. This defeatist attitude was uncharacteristic of Clark but, like all of us, he did have his off days.

The French Grand Prix saw him in a better frame of mind. Clark had a tremendous race with Giancarlo Baghetti who was driving a privately entered Ferrari, Dan Gurney in the works Porsche, and his team-mate Innes Ireland, but all were troubled by the heat and the stones which were flying around. Clark's goggles finally fell apart and, in fumbling for his reserve pair, he dropped out of the leader's slipstream and had to fight his way back to finish third. Baghetti beat everyone and, although it was not for want of trying, he never again came close to such fame.

In strict contrast came Aintree and the British Grand Prix, held in pouring rain. In these conditions Moss was brilliant but, like Clark, he was to retire from the race, leaving it a Ferrari benefit once more.

So the season progressed, and the only glimmer of hope for those outside the Ferrari stable came at the German Grand Prix when Jack Brabham arrived with a very special Cooper equipped with the new Coventry-Climax V8 engine. It produced 180 bhp and, though not quite up to the Ferraris, it was felt that the fact that the British cars were lighter and handled better would make sure that the extra 25 bhp would not be wasted. Moss in his Lotus was superb again in the damp and misty conditions, and he won the race with Clark in fourth.

Then came the Italian Grand Prix of 1961 — the race which would finally confirm the Ferrari supremacy and give a Ferrari driver the World Championship. That driver should have been Wolfgang von Trips who had driven brilliantly throughout the season, but what should have been his great triumph turned to tragedy.

Ferrari was determined to put on a show in front of his home crowd, and he entered five cars for von Trips, Phil Hill, Richie Ginther, Giancarlo Baghetti and Ricardo Rodriguez. Brabham had his V8 Climax engine for the Cooper, and Stirling Moss had also managed to get a V8, but neither used it in the race, and Clark was again well-placed against the Ferraris, thanks to a great deal of slipstreaming.

In fact it was slipstreaming which ultimately caused the accident to von Trips involving Clark. It happened at the braking point for the Vedano bend. The race had not long been under way and the Ferraris were already forging ahead, with von Trips slightly behind but charging through the field. He got past Clark and set out after Phil Hill, not realising that Clark had tagged along behind. Arriving at the braking point Clark decided to pull

Racing drivers in the 1960s were less flamboyant and seemed less under pressure than drivers today. This little group relaxing by the track includes a very young looking Jackie Stewart on the far left, South African driver Tony Maggs third from the left, with Sally Stokes and Jim Clark on his left.

out and overtake, relying on the lighter Lotus' ability to stop more easily than the Ferrari. Unfortunately, von Trips did not seem to notice this and, when Clark's front wheel came alongside the German's back wheel, they touched, Clark's car spinning violently anti-clockwise on to the grass and up a banking. Von Trips' car, on the other hand, spun right out of control, hit the fencing and overturned, throwing the driver out and killing him instantly, along with 14 spectators. Clark, badly shaken but unhurt, could only wander about, numbed by the enormity of the accident. Those must have been terrible moments for him as he realised what had happened. However, although he was dogged by various enquiries in Italy, which centred round the area of Italian law relating to responsibility in fatal accidents, he knew within himself that it was one of those tragic mistakes which inevitably happen in motor racing. Sadly it robbed motor racing of Wolfgang von Trips who had worked so hard to be World Champion, and gave the Championship to Phil Hill, the first American to win the title. I am sure that Phil would have preferred to win in different circumstances, for he was worthy of the Championship through his own driving ability.

For Clark the season faded away on a sour note when he finished a lowly seventh in the US Grand Prix; but at least he was able to see his team-mate Innes Ireland win the event and so give Colin Chapman his first Team Lotus victory in Grand Prix racing. A few weeks later Ireland was to leave the Lotus team and drive independently with the UDT Laystall team.

Clark was persuaded to make a December trip to South Africa where he drove in four races of which he won three, his new team-mate Trevor Taylor winning the fourth. This did a lot to restore Clark's confidence and taste for racing, and he began to prepare for the 1962 season in a better frame of mind.

The flexibility of the suspension of the Lotus Formula 1 car is well illustrated in these photographs of Clark in identical cars at Silverstone and Aintree. On full acceleration the car tended to rise up on its suspension, and on braking it plunged down, almost touching the track. By today's standards it was a very soft car, yet this fact didn't seem to affect Clark's driving.

Opposite *Both Jimmy Clark and Stirling Moss had a mutual regret: that they never raced against each other in competitive cars when each was at his peak. Each respected the other and this photograph, taken at East London, South Africa, has a poignant air with the new star, garlanded in victory, consoling the acknowledged finest British racing driver of his day.*

The Lotus 24 had been designed for the new Climax V8 and this too, like the others, was a tubular chassis design. But there was another new car in the pipeline — the Lotus 25 — the one which Clark would drive most frequently in his career.

By now the British teams had caught up with Ferrari, not only with the introduction of the Coventry-Climax V8 engine, but also with BRM's V8 with its characteristic battery of exhaust pipes sticking up in the air at the back. Again the pendulum swung towards chassis design and handling.

So, 1962 found the BRM and Lotus lined up to do battle with Ferrari. Clark's Lotus 25 was technically outstanding for that year in that it was a monocoque design, and it is interesting to look back and see that this now accepted form of designing a modern Grand Prix car was only introduced in 1962. Porsche too were out in force with new cars and their eight-cylinder engine, so it looked like being a close season. The Climax engine was now producing just over 180 bhp and was being used by a number of teams, including Cooper and Lola.

There were to be many highlights in 1962, not least of which was the possibility of Clark becoming World Champion in only his third season in Grand Prix racing. The first Grand Prix of the year took place as late as May at Zandvoort and, by that time, a lot of the bugs had been worked out of the new engines.

In the Dutch race it was Clark in the Lotus V8 and Gurney in the Porsche who led the way, but on the 11th lap Clark's gearbox gave trouble and he dropped back. Gurney had the same trouble with his Porsche, and Graham Hill came through brilliantly in his BRM to win his first ever Grand Prix. The Ferraris were disappointing; Phil Hill was back in the fourth row of the grid.

After Zandvoort Clark had a memorable race at the Nürburgring 1,000 km, the first appearance of the Lotus 23 — a twin-cam, 1,100 cc sports racing car. He led on the first lap, finishing it almost a minute ahead of the field, and had extended his lead over the Ferraris to 2½ minutes when the fumes from a broken exhaust manifold overpowered him and he ran off the road. His car was hidden so thoroughly in the shrubbery that the mechanics couldn't find it!

At Monaco it looked like being the same story as Zandvoort for, after a multiple accident at the first corner, Bruce McLaren was overtaken by Graham Hill in the BRM. Then Clark got going and he broke the lap record with regularity, first picking off McLaren and then closing on Hill. Together they broke the circuit record, but Clark just could not get past the flying Hill; the circuit took its toll on the gearbox and Clark again retired. The pressure had been too much for Hill also, for his car ground to a halt and he too was out, leaving the race to Bruce McLaren.

Next it was back to Spa. There seemed no doubt that Clark would win, even though Graham Hill had set up the fastest time in practice and Clark was way back in the fifth row of the grid. Somehow one knew that this time nothing could go wrong. By the end of the first lap Clark was up to fourth place — an incredible performance. A lap later he was fifth, then up to fourth again, then down to fifth, before he made a superhuman effort on the seventh lap to take second place and one lap later the lead which he held right to the end, setting a new lap record at 133.98 mph. This exciting race had provided Clark with the first of the four victories he was to achieve in the Belgian Grands Prix.

In the French Grand Prix a suspension ball joint pulled loose and Clark was out when in the lead.

At the British Grand Prix at Aintree Clark was out to follow up his earlier success in the Aintree 200, and he led the race almost all the way, setting a new lap record, and lapping all but three of the field.

The German Grand Prix had an ominous beginning. He stalled his car on the start line and lost 13 seconds on the field in getting away. But once again we were treated to one of his brilliant performances as he passed 16 cars on the opening lap and eventually finished fourth, despite problems with fuel.

By now Clark was in a strong position in the World Championship table, and in the Italian Grand Prix, despite his forebodings about the Monza circuit, he looked like adding some more points to his already impressive total. After rocketing into the lead from the start, he was only half-way round the circuit when the gearbox started to tighten up again and, after a pit stop, he retired, leaving Graham Hill to win in his BRM and so giving him a commanding lead in the championship.

Time was running out now, and the US Grand Prix saw Clark and Hill in contention again, with Clark holding out this time to win the race by a short head. One Grand Prix race remained, the South African at Kyalami, and

Opposite *Racing cars have changed considerably during the past decade. This odd-angled photograph shows the first of the Climax-V8-engined Formula 1 Lotuses at the Nürburgring. The development which was to see low diameter, wide-tread tyres had not yet begun.*

At Silverstone in 1963 Clark cocks his head in characteristic fashion going into Club corner. The Lotus Climax at that time put very little rubber on the road compared with today's Grand Prix tyres.

everything rested on it. A win by Clark and the title was his, a win by Hill and he would take the title. Hill had the edge on Clark by virtue of three wins and two second places, so all the pressure was on Jimmy. In practice Clark was in tremendous form and broke the lap record for the circuit no less than 24 times. When it came to the race, Innes Ireland took the lead and Hill had wheelspin, but Clark quickly drew ahead and set off hell for leather. He led from Hill for 62 laps and the championship looked as though it was in the bag. Suddenly there was a puff of oil smoke which grew into a cloud and, when Clark came in, it was found that a bolt had fallen out of the distributor drive housing, leaving a hole for the oil to leak through: he was out of the race. Despite his disappointment Clark was the first to congratulate Graham Hill on his win.

During 1962 Clark had driven an Aston Martin DB4 Zagato in a couple of races, and Border Reivers had long since sold their Aston Martin DBR1 and had now disbanded their team. Clark never again raced in Scotland, although he made one or two guest appearances. Colin Chapman guarded Clark so jealously that there were few occasions when he was loaned to other teams.

Now there was no stopping Clark and Chapman. It could be said that, in 1962, Clark had been robbed of victory by a series of mechanical failures, but there was no doubt that he was out to win the 1963 championship, and to win it handsomely.

The Lotus 25 was again the chosen car in 1963, and the Climax V8 engine was becoming more and more reliable. This year, as in 1962 and 1961,

Monaco proved to be Clark's nemesis, and it started off the Grand Prix year on a bad footing. Again Clark and Hill shared the front row of the grid, and this time it was Hill who took the lead, only to be passed by Clark who was in turn repassed by Hill. The crowd knew they were in for a humdinger of a motor race. Yet again Clark went into the lead, and this time it seemed to be for keeps until, with a 14-second lead, he found no gears in the gearbox at the Tabac corner and coasted down to the hairpin where the lever eventually selected not just one but two gears, jamming the gearbox. This let Graham Hill, the World Champion, take over once again to win the Monaco Grand Prix.

Belgium was a different kettle of fish. Despite pouring rain towards the end of the race, Clark ran away and hid from everyone else; at one stage he had lapped the entire field, but then he eased off towards the end to let second-place man Bruce McLaren unlap himself in the Cooper. In Holland it was the same happy story, despite a little fracas with the police when he was alleged to have stood in the wrong place with the wrong pass during practice. On his way to winning the race he once again lapped the whole field, becoming the first man to lap Zandvoort at more than 100 mph into the bargain.

France saw another victory, despite a halting engine which caused him some problems. At Silverstone for the British Grand Prix the story was repeated with Clark quickest in practice. In the early stages of the race the

Jimmy Clark was a past master on the Nürburgring, and this typical action picture of him on one of the many jumps at the circuit illustrates the great demands put on modern Grand Prix cars by some of the traditional circuits designed before the War.

two Brabhams of Dan Gurney and Jack Brabham led until passed by Clark, who then pulled away to win by 35 seconds from Surtees in the Ferrari. Clark now had a clear lead in the championship with 36 points to Ginther's 14 in the BRM.

His rivals' rot stopped at the Nürburgring where John Surtees put in one of his brilliant performances to win for Ferrari. Although Clark was first off the line, he was passed by Ginther and McLaren on the way round the first

Above left and above *Though normally placid, there were times when Clark showed his border fighting spirit, such as at the Dutch Grand Prix in 1963 when he walked over to a corner to watch his colleagues practising. A Dutch policeman did not recognise Clark and accused him of not carrying the correct pass. A scuffle followed and Clark was marched off, only to be released after lengthy explanations.*

Left *In a more playful mood, he fakes his displeasure at Colin Chapman, making an unexpected lunge. Chapman proves that he is no Muhammad Ali.*

lap and, before it was completed, Surtees had passed into second place, while Clark had gone ahead of McLaren. On the second lap Surtees took over the lead and Clark passed Ginther into second place. After some tremendous driving by both men, Clark passed Surtees, but he couldn't pull away from the Ferrari, and eventually Surtees went ahead when the Lotus went off song. Surtees won his first Grand Prix race and Clark took second; he still led the championship.

Monza was decisive. Clark had not only Surtees to contend with but Graham Hill and Dan Gurney too. Surtees took the lead first, and when he dropped a valve Clark took over from him, only to be passed by Gurney. The two of them switched places for the rest of the race, but in the end Clark triumphed: his fifth Grand Prix win of the season, and a victory which put the World Championship beyond doubt. His triumph was tarnished a little, however, as the Monza incident of 1961 had still not been settled, and the whole matter was brought up again, causing even more anguish.

In the US Grand Prix Clark's battery was flat, and he lost a lap and a half at the start before setting out to catch up. As usual, he thrust his way through the field at tremendous speed, setting a new lap record in the process and finishing third to Graham Hill and Richie Ginther in their BRMs. In Mexico Clark kept up the pressure, although the championship had been decided long before, and he won the race brilliantly. Just to make certain, he took his seventh Grand Prix victory in South Africa in December, a record which has never been beaten by any Grand Prix driver in a single season.

As if this were not enough Clark visited Indianapolis during 1963 and came close to winning the Indianapolis 500. In so doing he started a revolution there, affecting a whole sphere of motor sport which had seen no great European influence for many decades.

Apart from single-seaters, Clark had also driven the Lotus Cortina in 1963 and had once tried a Ford Galaxie at Brands Hatch — more for fun than for profit. He also became a more regular traveller to the United States, using a Lotus 23 and a banger of a Lotus 19 in two races in California.

Clark and the Lotus Cortina at Brands Hatch.

From now on, season followed season with a similar pattern. At the end of
1963 he didn't go to the Tasman series and so had a reasonably quiet time
until the new season started, when he raced a Lotus Cortina and the Lotus
25, and took in Formula 2 racing also. At the April 1964 Oulton Park
meeting he took three wins in three different cars (Lotus Cortina, Lotus Elan
and Lotus 19), and a week later he drove the Lotus 25, 30 and Cortina at
Aintree with slightly less success.

The 1964 season was to prove a particularly busy one for Clark with all his
commitments; his new contract with Ford meant that he was more often seen
in the Lotus Cortina, as well as being involved in Ford promotions.

Once again the Grand Prix season started with the Monaco Grand Prix,
and this time Clark at least managed to finish, but there was no concealing
his disappointment in again failing to win what he admitted was his favourite
race. This time he flew into the lead and clipped a bollard which loosened the

*Throughout his racing career, from the earliest days in Scotland, Jackie Stewart had a true
friend in Jim Clark. Clark did a great deal to persuade people that Jackie had tremendous
potential. This photograph was taken at Brands Hatch in 1964, with Stewart at the wheel of
the Ecurie Ecosse Tojeiro-Ford. The driver on the left is BOAC pilot Hugh Dibley, who
competed in sports car racing.*

Jimmy Clark on the hairpin at Spa, on his way to setting a record of four wins in the Belgian Grand Prix. This was his second victory in a Grand Prix using the new Ford engine.

rear anti-roll bar. He called into the pits to have it removed and went back to drive brilliantly into fourth place. In Holland he won again, and it looked like a repeat performance of 1963.

Clark's luck held and he won the Belgian Grand Prix after Graham Hill and Dan Gurney ran out of fuel and Bruce McLaren had broken his battery. It was undoubtedly his luckiest win. Clark was leading again in the French Grand Prix on the Rouen circuit, but this time he blew a piston and Gurney won. At the British Grand Prix it was back to Clark, who had a race-long battle with his arch-rival Graham Hill. This put Clark back in the lead in the championship, but at Nürburgring it was Surtees' day again, Clark retiring with another engine failure — this time a dropped valve.

The Austrian Grand Prix which followed was held on a rough circuit, and it was evidently going to be won by the strongest car, in this case Bandini's Ferrari. For Clark it was another retirement, due to a broken half-shaft, and the championship looked like evaporating before his eyes. As Monza the sorry tale continued with another engine failure and a win for John Surtees. Graham Hill and Jim Clark were now the closest contenders to Surtees. In the US Grand Prix Clark looked unbeatable, but the gremlins were still out in force: the fuel injection acted up and he was sidelined yet again. Hill won the race and so took the lead from Surtees with one race to go. It was all or nothing again, just as in 1962.

In the rare atmosphere of Mexico City fuel was going to play an important part. When the flag came down Clark took the lead, leaving his two rivals somewhere behind. The first signs of trouble came with a trace of oil on the track, so Clark moved his line and the oil followed him. This time it was a rubber pipe fracture and with every lap his precious oil drained away, along

The same scene, two years apart. Jimmy Clark in his Lotus prior to starting the Belgian Grand Prix at Spa in 1963, and just leaving the pits for the start of the same race at the same circuit in 1965. He won the race four times and yet hated the circuit more than any other, hence the apparent apprehension.

In the mid-1960s sports car racing turned to using the big American V8 engines and this was what Jimmy Clark had been waiting for. He had always loved big hairy sports cars, and Colin Chapman introduced first the Lotus 30 and then the Lotus 40. Even Clark was a bit dubious about the handling of the Lotus 40, but he drove it in some very spirited races. At Oulton Park it was John Surtees in his Lotus-Chevrolet who led the race from Bruce McLaren's early McLaren. Clark in car No 4 took an outside line in the Lotus 40.

In the same race he got to grips with the 40 and is seen on the fast section to Clearways corner. Some idea of the acceleration of the car can be gained by noting the height of the nose as compared with the tail as Clark puts his foot hard down.

with his chances of retaining the World Championship. By taking second place to Dan Gurney, John Surtees became the 1964 World Champion.

If 1964 had been one disappointment after another, 1965 was probably Clark's greatest year, capped by his triumph at Indianapolis. In 1964 tyre trouble had forced him out of the race, but this time he made sure of victory, winning at a new record speed.

In 1965 the South African Grand Prix became the first, rather than the last, event of the year, taking place on January 1. It saw the Grand Prix racing debut of Clark's friend Jackie Stewart, the man who was to take over Jimmy's reputation as the 'flying Scotsman'. Clark won the race easily, and Stewart took his first World Championship point by finishing sixth.

The past frustrations of Monaco were forgotten in 1965, as neither Clark nor Lotus took part, their main effort being concentrated on Indianapolis. Graham Hill won Monaco once more, as if to give Clark warning of the battle to come.

Back in Europe after his Indy victory, Clark went to Spa and triumphed again, making it four wins in a row. To make it even sweeter it was Jackie Stewart who followed him home in the BRM.

Jackie cheekily took the lead in the French Grand Prix at Clermont Ferrand, but Clark powered past him and won as he pleased. At the British Grand Prix he won again, despite taking it easy in the closing laps because of a shortage of oil. The 1965 World Championship seemed to be secure.

At Zandvoort the story was the same — another win — though all did not run smoothly, since Chapman ended up in jail, accused of assaulting a policeman who had tried to curb his enthusiasm. It would not have been surprising if the other drivers had accused Chapman of assault with a

Saloon car racing was always great fun, and whenever Clark drove the Lotus Cortina there were rarely more than three wheels on the ground. In one picture he is seen cornering hard at Oulton Park at Island Bend, while in the other he has the car at full stretch on the downhill Bottom Bend at Brands Hatch. Both cars were works cars in 1965.

deadly weapon, as Clark seemed to be invincible! With his usual determination he was out to win everything in sight, as if to lay low the 1964 gremlins.

The Nürburgring is a circuit Clark loved: a driver's circuit. Once again he was first away at the start and drove his heart out, setting not only a new track record, but also a new race record, making it six Grand Prix wins in a row.

At Monza the winning streak came to a halt. Stewart led from the start with Clark behind him, but later the tables were turned and Clark galloped ahead. He didn't have it all his own way this time, however, as both Stewart and Hill challenged him all the way. Then John Surtees came along in his Ferrari and took the lead, only to find that his gearbox went sour. Then Clark also headed for a permanent pit stop when the fuel pump ceased working. It was Jackie Stewart who went on to win this Grand Prix: the first win of a record-breaking career.

In the US Grand Prix Clark never looked like winning, and Graham Hill brought home the bacon. The season ended with the Mexican Grand Prix where Richie Ginther in the Honda Grand Prix car surprised everyone with a win. For Clark it was an odd experience, everyone seemed to pass him on the straight on the opening lap, leaving him in eleventh place. He managed to pull up to seventh, but the Climax engine gave the death rattle and expired. Nevertheless, the World Championship was again his. For the duration of the 1½-litre formula Clark had proved to be the dominant driver, winning the World Championship twice and narrowly losing it on two other occasions.

For 1966 there was a new formula, for 3-litre cars, and not only that, Coventry Climax withdrew from Grand Prix racing; Chapman was going to have to start from scratch again.

One of Clark's finest races was his attempt to win the Monaco Grand Prix in 1966. He was driving a Lotus Climax with a small 2-litre engine and, as was always the case at Monaco, he was well placed when the car retired.

Top *Clark very rarely made mistakes, and this picture of him going wide on the grass at Brands Hatch during the 1966 British Grand Prix is uncharacteristic.*

Above *In the same race, the 1966 British Grand Prix, Clark displays the relaxed confidence of a man who could pace his car perfectly. He has just come out of the slow Stirlings bend, and is slightly oversteering right to the edge of the track.*

Everyone began the search for engines and, once again, the British teams were relatively unprepared. At Monaco Cooper were using an uprated version of Maserati's 2.5-litre V12 sports car engine, McLaren were using a destroked version of the 4.2-litre V8 Ford engine, while Jack Brabham was using a 3-litre Australian Repco engine, based on the Oldsmobile aluminium unit. Even Ferrari were in trouble, as only Surtees had a 3-litre (Bandini using a 2.4), and BRMs were using 2-litre V8s. In Clark's case the engine was a stroked 2-litre version of the Climax he had used before, and this was relatively underpowered.

In the race Surtees led, chased by Stewart in his BRM; Clark had to claw his way up to third before retiring with suspension trouble.

Jim Clark's racing career

One of the most impressive motor sporting performances put up by Jim Clark was on the RAC rally in 1966. This took place at a time when the Scandinavians were dominating rallying, and when rally drivers felt that racing drivers could never be competitive in rallies and vice versa. Clark had rallied before he started racing, but he wanted to compete in a special stage event, so Ford Motor Company arranged for him to drive a factory Ford Lotus Cortina in the 1966 RAC.

Prior to this Clark did some serious practising with Ford's leading rally star Roger Clark. Roger and Jimmy became good friends, and Jimmy was able to try out his skill as a photographer. Clark's sheer enthusiasm for the event can be seen where he demonstrates with vigorous arm movements his technique on some of the corners at Bagshot where the testing took place. The man with the clip-board is Brian Melia, one of Britain's best co-drivers and a successful rally driver in his own right. It was he who took the co-driver's seat with Clark on the rally.

During the rally, in which Clark started in car No 8, Jimmy got quicker and quicker until his driving astonished even the Swedes. However, when he arrived in his native Scotland things began to go wrong.

Above Here he checks into the Bathgate control with Major Bob Tennant Reid, organiser of the International Scottish Rally, for a well-earned breakfast.

Left A few hours later, on Loch Achray special stage, Clark lost control on a downhill bend and hit the banking hard. This broke a front strut and severely mauled the coachwork, and Ford mechanics got down to the repair work in Aberfoyle village.

Jim Clark's racing career

Right *A rather chastened Jim Clark and Brian Melia look on with the locals as the work goes on. Former Ford rally driver and competitions manager Henry Taylor stands between them.*

Below *Meanwhile, out in the Loch Ard stage which immediately followed, the spectators waited patiently, none more so than a short-haired Jackie Stewart who came along to watch Clark in action.*

Right *Finally the car was patched up and, despite severe body damage on Clark's side, the World Motor Racing Champion put up a brilliant performance until he went off in the Scottish borders and had to retire. It was typical of him that, after retiring, he borrowed another car and helped to service the remaining Fords on the rally.*

Lotus had ordered the new BRM H16 engines but, behind closed doors, Ford were working on a new 3-litre V8 engine of their own, and Lotus appeared to be the likely customers.

In Belgium Clark's run of victories on the Francorchamps circuit came to an end, as he was left on the grid with the mechanics still around him. His enthusiasm to catch the pack when he eventually did get started blew the engine before he had travelled any distance. Meanwhile, up front, the leaders hit heavy rain, and Jackie Stewart spun out, suffering his only major accident in motor racing. This left John Surtees out in front to drive brilliantly in the wet to win for Ferrari.

In the French Grand Prix the BRMs now had the H16, but used the 2-litre engines as they were unsure of the reliability of the 3-litre. It was in this race that Clark was hit in the eye by a bird and retired, while Jack Brabham with his Brabham-Repco stormed ahead and won. By the British Grand Prix the World Championship was wide open but, when Brabham went out and won again, leaving Clark to finish fourth after a pit stop for brake fluid, the writing was on the wall.

There was still no news of the H16 BRM engines when it came to the Dutch Grand Prix, and Clark was once more driving the Lotus with the underpowered Climax engine. Things looked up, however, as Clark had one of his flying starts and took the lead as far as the Tarzan bend, where Brabham took over. A lap later Hulme had also overtaken him. After a few more laps Clark managed to retake Hulme and caught and passed Brabham to take the lead once more. It didn't last, however, for Brabham used his superior power to overtake Clark again. Then Jimmy's water pipe sprung a leak and he had to make a pit stop, letting Graham Hill into second place. Clark eventually finished third, just ahead of Stewart.

By the time it came to the German Grand Prix Clark had given up all hope of winning the championship again, as it seemed impossible for him to be competitive without more power. Despite this he was one of eight drivers inside the 1965 outright lap record for the Nürburgring, and at the start it

One of the few occasions when Jim Clark was injured during his racing career was at Cortina in Italy, when Ford laid on a junket to celebrate the Ford Cortina. In this impromptu snowball fight Clark injured his back. On the right is Ford rally driver Eric Jackson, and on the left is East African Safari winner Peter Hughes.

was John Surtees — now driving for Cooper — who took the lead, with Clark in fourth place. Brabham soon went through, leaving Surtees and newcomer Jochen Rindt, in another Cooper-Maserati, to hold second and third. Clark was overtaken by Gurney, and he dropped a further place when Graham Hill went through. Eventually, when he was trying hard to regain his ground, he slid off the road and went out of the race. With yet another win under his belt there seemed nothing to stop Brabham from taking the World Championship.

At Monza Clark finally got his H16 BRM engine, so that he was on the same terms as Hill and Stewart with their BRMs. Clark was third on the front row of the grid, and was obviously happier with his engine than the other two were with theirs. Again Clark was left at the grid, but he set out with his usual determination, threading his way through the field. When up with the front runners, however, he lost a balance weight from one wheel and called into the pits. Finally the gearbox gave up the ghost and Clark was out. Ludovico Scarfiotti turned out to be the winner in his Ferrari, with Michael Parkes in second place in another Ferrari.

The only oasis in an arid season came in the US Grand Prix at Watkins Glen when everything went well for Clark with the H16 BRM-engined Lotus. Brabham was leading Clark when he got into trouble with a broken timing chain, and Clark swept through to win his only Grand Prix of the year and, incidentally, the only Grand Prix won by an H16 BRM-engined car. In the final race in Mexico Clark again had transmission trouble with the H16 Lotus and retired, leaving John Surtees in the Cooper-Maserati to bring a very frustrating season to a close. Another frustrating time for Clark in 1966 was Indianapolis, where he finished second to Graham Hill after the race had seemed buttoned up for him.

If 1966 had been futile for Clark, 1967 was decisive in pointing the way in

During the 1967 Grand Prix season Clark had the new Ford Cosworth engine, the brainchild of Keith Duckworth (centre) who worked closely with Chapman (right) and Clark.

which the 3-litre formula was going to go. The answer was provided by the Ford Motor Company, who had invested £100,000 in the development of a Grand Prix engine to take over where Coventry Climax had left off. This engine was to do all that was expected of it — and more.

The first event of what was to be Clark's last full Grand Prix season took place in South Africa, and for this race Clark was again using the BRM H16 engine, joined by Graham Hill, his new team-mate. Ironically, after all those years as close rivals, Hill and Clark were now together in the one team. It was a hot day with high track temperatures — tyre wear was going to be a crucial factor. Denny Hulme was leader on the opening lap with Clark down in fifth. Clark couldn't hold this position for long, however, as the car began to overheat, and in those temperatures no amount of slowing down was going to help matters. Finally the fuel pump packed up and Clark retired, the final verdict going to Pedro Rodriguez in a Cooper-BRM.

Ferrari had missed South Africa and appeared at Monaco with a new engine, while Stewart ditched the H16 BRM for an old 2-litre V8. Clark and Hill also went for smaller engines; Clark opted for a 1,916 cc Climax, and Hill chose the 2-litre V8 BRM for his Lotus. Obviously Lotus were desperate for their new engine.

Although Clark didn't finish, the South Africa Grand Prix was one of his truly outstanding races. He spun the car early on in the race and consequently had to work his way up from the back. In so doing he broke the lap record and eventually reached third place. His just deserts for this fine effort were not forthcoming, however, for, while in third place, he spun yet again and retired on the spot.

At Zandvoort, scene of so many of Clark's triumphs, the tables turned again and the Ford V8 engine was rolled out in the Lotus 49. This was an

At Zandvoort in 1967 Jim Clark appeared for the first time with the Ford Cosworth engine and dominated the race. Here he leads Denny Hulme in his Brabham. It was the start of a new era in motor racing as the Cosworth engine is still winning Grand Prix races today.

Before the start of the Belgian Grand Prix in 1967, the last time he raced at Spa, Clark strolls nonchalantly about the pits while the police clear the crowds.

entirely new combination, and one which was to start a revolution in Grand Prix racing. Clark had minor trouble with wheel bearings and was low on the grid, but team-mate Graham Hill was on pole position in a similar Ford-engined car. Hill led everyone on the first lap, with Clark soon worrying his way through the field to fourth. Hill broke a camshaft drive, so Brabham took over the lead, with Rindt right behind and Clark up next. Within 16 laps, however, Clark had passed them both and was in the lead, a lead which he held to the end. He felt as though a weight had been lifted off his shoulders: he had a winning car again.

Belgium looked as though it was going to consolidate Clark's Zandvoort success, as it saw him out in front lapping at more than 150 mph. He was timed at more than 190 mph on the straight, but it didn't last, as he pulled into the pits with a plug failure and returned to the field in eighth place. He had to return to the pits with the same trouble later, and Dan Gurney won with his Eagle.

The French Grand Prix was run that year at Le Mans, and it proved to be a boring GP circuit. Clark was on the front of the grid, and it was Graham Hill who was first away; but not for long, as Clark took the lead after six laps and pressed on. On the 22nd lap his transmission failed and Clark was out.

Clark could have been forgiven for thinking that it was going to be 'another of those seasons', but the British Grand Prix at Silverstone demonstrated once again that the Clark-Lotus-Ford package was the one to beat, and he won his fifth British Grand Prix. In Germany Clark led again, but the

Above *Lotus were relatively unprepared for the first season of the 3-litre formula, and they used various engines during the 1966 season. Clark created history by being the only person to win a Grand Prix using the BRM H16 Grand Prix engine: this was the American Grand Prix that year. A few weeks later, at the Mexican Grand Prix, Clark, still using the BRM H16 engine, was put out with transmission trouble. The photograph was taken early in the race.*

Opposite *Clark's last major Championship win was in the Australian/New Zealand Tasman series of 1967. In many of his races that winter he came up against the New Zealander Chris Amon in his Ferrari, and here they are pictured side by side on the starting grid. Clark's car had already been painted in the Gold Leaf Lotus red and gold for the 1968 season.*

handling went awry, and eventually he retired with deranged suspension. The race was won by Denny Hulme who was well on the way to winning his first World Championship for Brabham.

In Canada we had the same story, with Clark out in front in the wet until he was passed by Hulme, then Clark retook the lead when the rain began to fall more heavily, only to have his engine die on him, and he retired yet again. Then came Monza and another of Clark's great races. Though not first away, Clark led after five laps only to be passed by Hulme, who in turn was repassed by Clark, who then dived into the pits with a puncture. In this company and at such high speeds it looked as though it was all over for Clark, but he smoked out of the pits, once more a lap behind, and began to go motor racing. Two laps from the end he did the impossible and took the lead again, only to run short of fuel and have to call in the pits again, letting Surtees through to win the race for Honda.

In the American Grand Prix Clark and Hill had tossed a coin to see who would win, as it seemed certain that nothing could touch the Lotus-Fords. As it turned out Hill led with Clark second, but Hill's car started to run sick, so Clark took over and won, apologising to Hill for spoiling the plan. In Mexico it again looked to be all Clark's way, despite the fact that he had an eventful practice session caused by bad handling. He was on pole position of the grid

and, when the starter hesitated, Clark hesitated also, and found himself rammed by Gurney, an incident which eliminated the American but which, fortunately, sent Clark on his way undamaged. Graham Hill led the race initially, but on the third lap Clark came through to lead, determined to get as far ahead of Chris Amon in the Ferrari as possible. With Denny Hulme taking third place, the Championship was his, but Clark had won the last race, equalling Fangio's record number of Grand Prix wins.

The 1967 Indy was Clark's last — although he practised for the 1968 event

Left *On this occasion he made a mistake and slid on to the grass in the Levin Grand Prix in New Zealand.*

Below *A typical action picture of Jimmy Clark during the Tasman series, turning on the power of his Ford Cosworth engine and oversteering out of the corner.*

in a Lotus Turbine two weeks before he was killed — and he finished a lowly 31st, not a very pleasing result for him.

During the last winter Clark had a victorious time in the Tasman series, winning it hands down. It was a fine preparation for the 1968 season.

By now things had changed. Stewart had despaired of BRM and had joined forces with Ken Tyrell in a Matra, which looked promising. Everyone was getting to grips with the 3-litre formula so that it looked like being a good season. Lotus had taken on a sponsor in Gold Leaf cigarettes and, although

Above *Clark in action in the Levin Grand Prix before going off the road.*

Right *Jim Clark was willing to drive anything if the car proved to be sufficiently interesting, and on one of his trips to California he tried this typical American Midget racer.*

Jimmy Clark's last Grand Prix win in the South African Grand Prix of 1968 gave him tremendous pleasure as he had broken the record held by Juan Manuel Fangio of the largest number of wins in Grand Prix races. Clark's record was to stand for five years until it was broken by Jackie Stewart driving his Tyrell Ford.

Above and opposite *In these pictures Jimmy Clark drives past the photographers on his way to the lap of honour. The laurel wreath round his shoulders, Clark smiles contentedly.*

Clark had used the Gold Leaf livery in Australia, his car was a normal green and yellow Lotus for the first race of the year in South Africa. On the second lap of this race Clark took the lead, and he led to the finish, setting a new lap record.

It was Clark's 25th Grand Prix win and he had broken Fangio's long-standing record. Alas, also, it was to be his last.

In March he was at Indianapolis testing the Lotus Turbine and, later that month, he raced the Formula 2 Lotus 48 at Barcelona where he was rammed by Jackie Ickx. One week later, in damp and drizzly weather, he was running down the field in another Formula 2 race, this time at Hockenheim, when he suddenly skidded off the road on one of the quickest sections of the track and was killed.

Chapter 2

Back home in Indiana

I am willing to wager that, had not Jack Brabham taken one of his Grand
Prix cars into the hallowed portals of Indianapolis in 1961 and done
remarkably well, Dan Gurney might not have taken this a stage further and
persuaded Colin Chapman and Ford to get together and build an Indy-
winning rear-engined car. In turn, had Chapman not been convinced that
there was a chance of victory, then Clark surely would not have gone to
Indianapolis, for nothing was further from his mind than the annual American classic. One could be dramatic and say that Indianapolis changed his life;
whether this is true or not, it certainly changed his attitude towards racing in
general and towards Americans in particular.

I always had the feeling that, in the early days, Jimmy was ill at ease in the
United States. He would come back confused, feeling that the Americans
didn't really want to know about Europeans, for the plain and simple reason
that they had their own forms of racing and their attitudes were so different.
To Clark, taking part in American sports car racing on the West Coast was
like an English test cricketer going into major league baseball: the priorities
and attitudes were so different. He could never understand why so many
West Coast Americans went motor racing with scarcely a clue about how to
race a car: the sheer recklessness of sports car racing West-Coast style in
those days appalled him, and he often said that he raced there with both eyes
on the rear-view mirror. On occasion he got himself punted out on to the
grass, yet he kept going back, usually to drive cars which perhaps did not
match up to his ability, and for reasons which were best known to himself.

Dan Gurney had a feeling about the combination of rear-engined cars and
Indianapolis, and he became convinced that it must be the right one. But it
was not until 1962 that he really did something about it. He was driving for
Porsche that year, but when he saw Chapman's new Lotus 25 with its
monocoque chassis and obvious capabilities, he knew that he'd found the
answer. Despite the fact that he had accepted a drive from Mickey
Thompson in a rear-engined car of Thompson's design using a Buick V8
engine, Gurney persuaded Colin Chapman to go to Indianapolis to see the
race. It was enough; Colin saw the possibilities and he and Gurney started
work on an Indy car.

At about the same time some of the more enthusiastic engineers at Ford
began thinking that a Ford-engined win at Indianapolis might not be a bad
idea, as most people still seemed to be relying on the Offenhauser engine
which had dominated the race since before the War. A few weeks later, while
Ford were looking for a chassis in which to put a possible racing engine,
Chapman and Gurney arrived with their own ideas, and soon the deal was
fixed. Behind the scenes for the rest of the season Chapman worked on his
design while Ford worked on their engine. By October, when Clark had just

won the US Grand Prix at Watkins Glen in his Lotus, it was time to make the behind-the-scenes activity more public, so it was decided to take the Grand Prix car with its 1½-litre engine, producing only 175 bhp, down to Indianapolis for a try out.

It was this exploratory trip which made Clark slightly antagonistic towards Indianapolis because, give him his due, Clark had his pride, and you can imagine his feelings when he arrived to find that a number of veteran Indianapolis drivers had been tipped off and were there to see what the little European car was going to do. To Clark it was pretty dull because, after all, there was no one else on the track, and he had a car which on that circuit ran flat-out all the time. It was set up for a road circuit, and so the slightly banked anti-clockwise left-hand curves became a bit boring, but his fastest lap

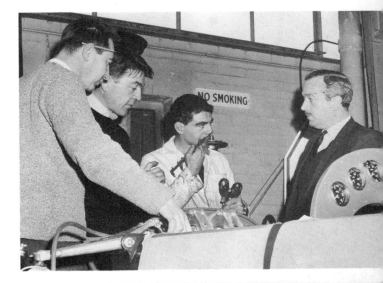

Early in 1963 Colin Chapman designed a new car to compete at Indianapolis. The work was done in a remarkably short time, and Chapman is seen on the right discussing the design with his mechanics at the Lotus factory.

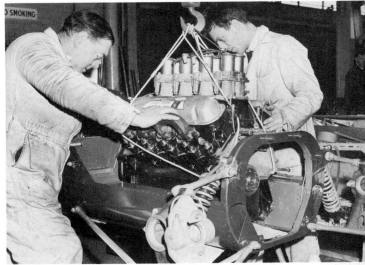

The first Ford V8 engine is lowered into the monocoque rear section of Jimmy Clark's 1963 Indianapolis Lotus. Compared to later years the engine was in a relatively minor state of tune.

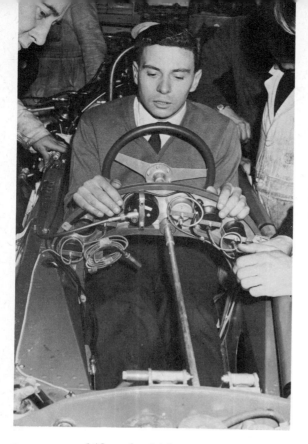

Once the engine had been fitted into the Indianapolis car and the cockpit completed, Jim Clark tried the car out for size. This picture taken at the Lotus factory shows just how little space there is in the cockpit of an Indianapolis car. On either side of Clark's legs are the fuel tanks, and in the normal driving position he would be lying back in the seat.

average was 143 mph which was pretty respectable for those days, even in a full-house Offenhauser, let alone with a 1½-litre Climax fire-pump engine.

The die was cast; the race was on. By February the first car had been completed and was tested at Snetterton, before being flown to Ford's private test track at Kingman, Arizona. As set up for Indianapolis the prototype, the Lotus 29, looked much like a normal Grand Prix car with a V8 engine and long exhaust stacks and, in the time between February 1963 and the race at the end of May, a great deal of work was done on it. For a start the engine was unreliable, and then the new version broke up on the test bench. Yet another revised engine was made up and taken down to Indianapolis for proper testing, where Dan Gurney unofficially became the second quickest man to lap the circuit. They were in business, and three cars were officially entered for the 1963 Indianapolis 500 with Clark one of the drivers, and Gurney the other (the third car was a spare).

The Indianapolis establishment had treated the Jack Brabham challenge two years before with benign, if somewhat amused patronage, but the Lotuses were something different. Suddenly nervous criticisms began to be voiced. There was a quibble about the special 15-inch tyres which Firestone made up for the Lotuses; the Americans didn't like the colour of the Lotuses, as green cars were an ill omen at the Speedway. Clark was asked to take a driver's test and bitterly resented the humiliation of having to run round Indianapolis at a slow speed, working his way up until he was informed that his driving was of a sufficient standard for him to be allowed to start the race. Practising when he was out on his own on the track always got him down badly, anyway. On one occasion he just pulled into the pits and went off to his hotel. He freely admitted that when he was out there on his own he had 'time to watch the wheels wobbling about and the walls, and I just kept frightening myself'.

All these little things got up Clark's nose, and the general hubbub and panjandrum which pertained to the Indianapolis publicity machine just didn't suit him. He came back from one trip particularly disgruntled as he had been having a rough time with the press. He felt they were being patronising and, when he reacted in typical Clark fashion, they didn't like it. He could not get used to people saying to him 'Hello Jimmy, glad to know you' — the standard greeting. It took him all his time not to explode and say 'But you *don't* know me!'

Behind all his outspoken distaste for what was going on, he was secretly pleased as punch with his performances on the track, and again we saw Clark replying to his critics in the way he knew best — out on the track in competition.

Reading contemporary reports of the first Indianapolis effort in 1963 it is obvious that Clark, Chapman and Ford didn't merit the success they had, because they were relatively unprepared. In one fell swoop they were bucking the tradition and, with the sanctity of innocence, they trod where tougher angels had feared to tread.

The race is now history, how Clark and Gurney dominated the race, how they saved a pit stop by running on petrol, rather than on a sophisticated alcohol-based fuel, and how Clark was beaten into second place after the leader, Parnelli Jones, had leaked oil.

Behind the scenes, however, things were different. Recalling the race

Dan Gurney, the man who conceived the idea of the Lotus Indianapolis effort, in the original prototype Lotus 29 during testing at Kingman, Arizona. At that time work had not yet begun on the tuning of the exhaust system which became an important factor in releasing more power from the engine.

today, Colin Chapman talks of the mounting tension in the Lotus pit for, with 30 laps after his second pit stop, Clark was obviously gaining on the leader, Jones.

'Jimmy was going quicker and quicker because his car was getting lighter, and he knew Jones had another pit stop on the cards, whereas he could drive to the finish. We worked out that he would catch Parnelli Jones 15 laps from the end of the race. We were delighted because we knew Parnelli couldn't go quicker and Jimmy was pressing hard. Jimmy had got within 3½ seconds of the leader, and in another three or four laps would have stormed past into the lead, but Jimmy suddenly stopped gaining and I must admit I found this rather unusual. I couldn't quite explain it because I couldn't see what the trouble was.' ·

The trouble was that Parnelli Jones was dropping a fair amount of oil on the track. Prior to the race all the drivers had been warned that, if they dropped just one speck of oil, they would be black-flagged and out of the race. Various people came to the Lotus pit and asked Chapman why he didn't demand the black flag, but Chapman felt he couldn't do this. After all, he was the underdog, and now he was about to beat the establishment at their own game. To have demanded the black flag was not good public relations and, anyway, he was totally convinced in his own mind that Jones could never finish if he was losing all that oil. But it continued, and Chapman got worried; he thought that the starter, Harlan Fengler, who had warned about oil, was turning a blind eye to the leader, and so Chapman went to see him. Fengler was standing with the black flag in one hand, but he was making no move to disqualify the leader. He kept saying that he wasn't sure that it was Jones' car which was at fault, even though the back of the car was covered in oil. Along came A. J. Agajanian, owner of Jones' car, and there was a film-set confrontation, with Fengler in his red fedora, looking up the track with the flag in his left hand, while Aganjanian in his white stetson parleyed. Beside him a track official studied Jones' car with binoculars, and Chapman, glowering with his fists clenched, stood at the back looking for all the world like the kid about to lose his toffee apple. Chapman made a decision which one suspects he regrets today. He decided to stand back and wait for Parnelli Jones' car to blow up, but it didn't, and Parnelli Jones won the 1963 Indianapolis 500.

Today Chapman admits that the race politics were beyond him at the time, and he realises that he should have kicked up a fuss and obliged Fengler to stick to the rules and disqualify Jones. Though the disappointment was great, he admits, as Clark did afterwards, that at least the team had shown the Americans the way ahead, and there is little doubt that Clark was the moral winner of the race. But that wasn't the end of the incident. Eddie Sachs — who was to be killed in a horrifying accident some years later — was bluntly outspoken: ' . . .If it would have been a fair race, a rookie Jim Clark would have won it, and I don't blame Parnelli, because he deserves to win. But I do blame the car owner [*Agajanian*]. Those officials shouldn't use politics. Everyone should be treated alike.'

Fengler, when asked why he didn't black-flag the car, explained that Agajanian and his chief mechanic, Johnny Pouelsen, had told him the trouble was a crack at the oil-tank hanger bolt, and that the oil had stopped leaking. This explanation had satisfied Fengler and he had let the car continue. Perhaps, with hindsight, Fengler did the right thing for, as

Indianapolis Star sports editor Jep Cadou Junior said, 'Had he [*Fengler*]
instructed Vidan [*the starter*] to black-flag Jones and thus cost him the race
there would have been a storm of protest that would have made the present
rhubarb look like a quiet hour in a monastery.'

Someone later commented that Fengler had once worked for the Ford
Motor Company and reckoned that he would have been accused of trying to
help out his former employer.

Jimmy's first Indianapolis 500 had been something of a traumatic experience. Talking about the race shortly afterwards he told me 'For me the
Indianapolis 500 was a landmark. There were times before the race when I
wished I hadn't been brought into it but, sitting back now and reflecting on
the race and the events which led up to it and the repercussions, it was one of
the most rewarding races I have ever had. It opened my eyes to many things
and, as a European with little real idea of what Indianapolis was all about, it
came as a big shock.

'If asked to describe Indy before I had been there I'd doubtless have said
that it was rather a phoney race, and in certain ways it is, but I really admire
the promoters who for months devote all their efforts to producing one of
the greatest, if not the greatest, motor racing spectacles in the world.'

As for the money involved, Colin Chapman claims that they only just
broke even on the 1963 Indy, as the contract he had with Ford USA was
based on a haphazard estimate of the likely cost involved. Indeed, Chapman,
Clark and Gurney dreamed up a wild figure in a cab when going to see Don
Frey, the Ford executive involved in the initial project, and asked for that
figure. As it transpired there were trips back and forward to the United
States for testing, the trials themselves, and all this proved to be far more
expensive than they had ever imagined. Second place brought in a substantial amount of money by European standards but, after paying the bills and
then splitting what remained, with 10 per cent to the mechanics and 45 per
cent each to the team and Clark, nobody walked away a millionaire.

Clark wasn't satisfied and still wanted to show America that he could beat
everyone in a straight race, so plans were made for him to compete in two
other events in the USAC Championship Trial that year: the Milwaukee 200
and Trenton.

'Nobody realised how important the Milwaukee race turned out to be,'
said Clark. 'Even A. J. Watson, the doyen of all Indianapolis car designers,
admitted after that race the front-engine roadster was finished.'

Milwaukee was very satisfying for Clark because not only did he win,
setting lap and race records on almost every lap, but he lapped the entire
field save one car, A. J. Foyt's roadster, and he freely admitted that to have
lapped Foyt would have been to rub things in a bit too much, so he held back
and crossed the line behind him.

Something of his determination to win this race came through in his
description of the start: 'I was in pole position and the starter had a yellow
and green flag. I had memorised the rules this time and, when I saw him
move his arm with the green flag, I was off in second gear. It was the first
time I had stamped hard on the accelerator in second gear with the Indy car,
for with 40 gallons of fuel aboard I knew it would grip like hell.

'Well, the first corner came up at me like a blur and my head was right back
in the headrest. I nicked it into third for the corner and held third round the
bend and down the back straight, so that I had a terrific lead at the end of the

The two drivers who led the Lotus assault on Indianapolis — Jim Clark photographed by Firestone in an uncharacteristic pose and Dan Gurney in his Indianapolis Lotus in 1964.

first lap.' For winning the race Clark picked up $12,000.

At this time Clark was still touchy about press reports, and he always felt that a newspaper should report winning and not losing. For instance, in the race at Trenton some weeks later, the steering broke on his Lotus, and the car smashed into the wall. All the British papers covered this incident, yet they had totally ignored the Milwaukee win, and this infuriated Clark. 'They give me big headlines because I run into the barrier, and here I am, fourth overall in the USAC Indianapolis Championship; no European driver has ever done that before.'

Sometimes Clark's aggression reached print, such as before the Trenton race when he boasted that he would ' . . .win the race and break the course record too'. At this his great rival, Parnelli Jones, who had beaten him at Indianapolis, replied 'Clark may go back to Scotland talking out of the other side of his mouth'. And he did; but only after he had led the race by half a lap, before a cheap little oil pipe came loose, letting all his precious oil spill away.

In 1964 Clark knew that he would win Indianapolis and set out to do so, leading the race until a tyre tread stripped, and only his tremendous skill and lightning reactions — plus a great deal of luck — saved him from disaster.

On this occasion Chapman had chosen to run Dunlop tyres rather than Firestones. These had to be made specially for the car, as Dunlop had not even looked at the problems of Indianapolis before. As a result they waited until the final time trial to see which compound and tread pattern was best, before actually making the race tyres. This in turn coincided with the

One of the most dramatic races for Clark at Indianapolis was when the team decided to run on Dunlop tyres. Due to a manufacturing fault they threw their treads, and Jim Clark displayed his cool mastery of race driving by holding a wild slide when the tread stripped off the tyre. The bald patch can be seen in this picture taken as Clark cooly drove back to the pits. The rear suspension, however, had been smashed in the process.

Whitsun holidays at Fort Dunlop. Possibly as a result of this and the general rush, the tread bonding, or curing, had not been done properly and the tread simply peeled off the tyre. In Clark's case the tyre failure wrecked the rear suspension on one side and he was out of the race. A check on Gurney's tyres showed that his were suffering from the same problem, and Chapman pulled Gurney out of the race.

Ford Motor Company were furious about this last action, and Chapman was summoned to Dearborn the next day to give his reasons. But the damage had been done; Chapman had withdrawn the cars without even consulting Ford who had put up the money. The party was over; the Ford/Lotus combine was through, as far as Indianapolis was concerned.

Some design work had already been done on a 1965 car, but this now seemed all washed up, so Chapman got down to planning the Grand Prix season. At the last minute, however, in February 1965, Ford came back with a set amount of money and certain commitments for the running of cars at Indianapolis, and Chapman and Clark were back once more on the Indianapolis trail.

By now the rear-engined cars had made their mark at Indianapolis — 17 of them were entered for 1965. Ford were now selling their Indianapolis engines to various people at $31,400 each, though they cut this figure by about $10,000 when they went into full production.

Despite all the last minute rush everything seemed to be going well for the

1965 effort. Jimmy had personal doubts and, even though he was under a separate driver's contract to Ford, he had seriously considered forgetting all about Indianapolis that year. Luckily this sheer determination to win the race after having come so close forced him to go. He even decided to miss the Monaco Grand Prix so as to concentrate on Indianapolis, despite having to sacrifice the chance of gaining Grand Prix championship points.

There was another reason compelling him to go to Indy. 'Lotus were going to Indianapolis whether I was there or not,' he recalled after the race, 'and I know the amount of effort and time that goes into Indianapolis. If Colin was going to spend all this time and effort on the Indy project, they were not going to put much effort into the Monaco Grand Prix, and I reasoned that I might as well be in on the thing they were concentrating on. Plus the fact that we had worked for three years to try and break this bloody place [*Indianapolis*]. Though it didn't get an obsession with me, it got to the stage where we had gone there the first year and we should have bloody well won that thing if we hadn't been so stupid in working out the yellow light system; and then the next year I am convinced I would have won it but for this tyre problem we had so, having missed the carrot both times, I decided to try and do it again.'

This was a much harder decision than one might think, for Indianapolis also meant for Jimmy another long wrangle with the press, but, although he complained most of the time about the way he was treated by them, there were occasions when he actually enjoyed the experience.

In 1965 everything went right for Jimmy, and he enthused about the car. 'It's beautiful. But you have to keep it up there and, coming out the corners at Indianapolis at 7,400 rpm or 7,500 rpm, it screams right up to about 9,000

The three Lotus-based cars in the 1965 race which were always in contention: A. J. Foyt's Sheraton-Thompson Special (1) on the inside; Jimmy Clark in the Lotus (82); and Dan Gurney in the All American Racers Special sponsored by Yamaha (17). Foyt was placed on pole position of the grid and led the race early on.

On his way to victory Clark passes Arnie Knepper driving his Konstant Hot Special, one of the old-style, front-engine Indianapolis cars.

rpm, and I was so scared stiff as it sounded as though it was going to blow asunder. I tell you, this thing at 9,000 rpm all screaming and banging and thumping around behind me is absolutely fantastic.'

Then there was the matter of A. J. Foyt. Jimmy had first met 'A.J.' some years before and had befriended him, but in 1964 Foyt had thumbed his nose at the Fords, and the relationship between the two of them had deteriorated considerably. A friend of Foyt's is alleged to have said before the race that 'A.J. would run with one wheel on top of the wall if he had to — to beat Jimmy Clark'.

Jimmy's side of the story was only slightly less aggressive. After setting fastest time in practice for pole position, Foyt had said 'I just wanted to bring the honor back to America', and Jimmy took this as a personal slur. In turn Jimmy thought that Foyt had prepared badly for the race, as he had over-loaded his car with extra fuel and was throwing too much strain on the transmission; as it turned out it was a transmission failure that put Foyt out of the race.

Jimmy was in the middle of the front row of the grid, and he started the race as he meant to finish it — out in front. 'I took the lead from the start, which was an unprecedented thing, for I believe it is the first time anyone has taken the lead at the first bend from anywhere other than pole position. Mind you, that was a statistic which nobody would confirm, which was strange as they are always quoting statistics at you.

'I held the lead through the first lap and on the second Foyt was right behind me, and I saw him pull out so I backed off, for I thought that if he wanted to run quicker than I did let him get on with it, remembering that he had tyre trouble in practice and he was with a full fuel load in the opening

Above *The moment of glory for Colin Chapman as Jimmy Clark crosses the line to win the 1965 Indianapolis, five miles ahead of his nearest competitor and at a record average speed of over 150 mph. Rushing towards Chapman with his back towards the camera is J. C. Agajanian, the entrant of the 1963 winner, Parnelli Jones.*

Opposite *The scene in Victory Lane after Clark won the race. The girl is Miss Indianapolis 1965, Suzanne Devine. Behind her Colin Chapman is interviewed for radio.*

laps really powering it on. If ever he was going to have trouble it was going to be driving like that. However, I found he was just slowing me down, so I repassed him in an effort to make him come out after me.

'I realised things were going well just after the first pit stop. I went back out on to the track to find Parnelli Jones in front of me and I wasn't sure if he had had his pit stop or if he hadn't so I passed him. The pit gave me the sign "plus 58 Parnelli" so that was me a full lap ahead of him. I thought, Christ, that's good. A few laps later and we both shot past another car and I looked, only to find it was Foyt who was lumbering away from his pit stop, but he soon came

In 1966, after Graham Hill had won the Indianapolis 500, there was a party at his house, and as usual Jimmy Clark joined in the fun. Graham's son Damon is doing most of the pushing, while among the onlookers are Louis Stanley of BRM, Les Leston, Henry Taylor and the late Gregor Grant of Autosport.

charging up again so I let him past. The pit gave me the sign "plus 58 plus 58" which meant I was a lap ahead of both Parnelli and Foyt . . .after that, I knew we had won.'

At the end of the race Jimmy shot down the pit lane, almost collecting Colin Chapman who was doing his customary St Vitus' dance of victory. In the winner's circle Suzanne Devine, the 500 Festival Queen, pouted and kissed Clark's cheek, though *Time* magazine reported that he had politely shaken her hand. This I can't believe, even if his girl-friend Sally was in the crowd somewhere, trying to fight her way through to the front with Hazel Chapman.

The winner's spoils were pleasant — nearly $170,000 for overall and lap money, as well as the most unlikely prizes, such as free meat for a year from a local butcher (Jimmy took cash in lieu), and a $1,000 wardrobe from Dick Miller's man's store.

Having won in 1965 one might have been forgiven for thinking that it would be the end of Jim Clark's preoccupation with Indy but, in fact, he was to go back in 1966 and 1967, and he tested the Lotus Turbine with a view to racing it at Indy in 1968.

In 1966 Jimmy went back to Indianapolis to finish second to Graham Hill. This was a controversial race because there were several allegations that the official lap-scorers got their sums wrong, following a big accident on the opening lap. The race was stopped and restarted and, throughout the race, Colin Chapman and his lap-scorer and time-keeper, Cyril Audrey, were convinced that Clark was in the lead. But the scoreboard showed that Hill was in the lead and, following the race, Cyril Audrey spent nearly ten hours with the officials, going through the electronic tapes.

Despite the controversy, Graham Hill won the 1966 Indianapolis 500 with Jimmy second, and even that performance was outstanding, bearing in mind that Jimmy survived two enormous, gut-wrenching 140-mph spins during the race when he calmly lay back and steered his way out of trouble. In one of those spins, which would have kept most people well occupied, if not terrified, Jimmy even noticed Jackie Stewart pass him, waving an admonitory finger at his mistake, and grinning all over his face. It was this kind of thing that aroused the fans. This was class, and this was what marked Jimmy Clark out as someone special, even in the partisan eyes of the Indianapolis crowd.

In 1967 everything went wrong. The Indy car was designed to take a modified version of the BRM H16 Grand Prix engine and, when this was not available, it was chopped around in order to take another Ford engine. Ford was not backing the effort this time, and it was engine trouble which put Jimmy out of the race when lying a lowly 31st.

But in 1968 things were different. While Jimmy had been racing in his final Tasman series 'down under', Colin Chapman had been designing a new

The press reactions to the victory surprised even Jimmy Clark, who was no lover of headlines at other times. On this occasion, however, he didn't mind them in the least!

Flying Scot's £75,000 Indianapolis triumph

A FIRST FOR BRITAIN—CLARK WINS AT 150 mph

From TONY DELANO, Indianapolis, Monday

TAIN'S Jim Clark today became the irst Briton to win America's top motor t—the Indianapolis 500-mile race.

average speed for the race, which has claimed ix lives in forty-nine events, was a fantastic 86 m.p.h. — a record.

, who finished **FIVE MILES** ahead of his nearest rival, h a searing pace that only eleven cars out of thirty-inished.

arter of a million ered Clark, driving sh Lotus-Ford, to a victory will bring him at £75,000 in prize y and winners' together with an us silver trophy. lark drove sweat-stained into the ruit's Victory Alley

His car was surrounded by a 30-man pipe band blowing so hard that they drowned the engine scre from cars still finishing

Leading

The 29-year-old Scot, who was the 1963 world champion, is the first foreigner to win the race since Italy's

Of the eleven cars that finished, four were Lotus-Fords.

Clark was already leading by more than a minute —nearly a lap—in the 114th lap when his toughest opponent, Texan A. J. Foyt, dropped out with mechanical trouble.

Clark took the lead at the first corner. Foyt got it back for one lap but after that he saw nothing of the flying Scotsman but the yellow flared exhausts of his little Ford-engined, slipper-shaped green car.

Parnelli Jones, the tough Indianapolis veteran who beat Clark for first place in the 1963 race, was second.

Third was Mario Androtti, a young Italian on the track for the first time.

After the race, Clark said: "I feel great."

Lotus designer Colin Chapman said: "The only thing we were worried about was Foyt."

He need not have worried. Jim Clark would have won today even if he had to get out and refuel himself.

Above *After his second place in the 1963 Indianapolis 500, Jim Clark became something of a schoolboy hero to thousands of American boys. As a result of this Ford Motor Company in America produced this advertisement which appeared in various Sunday comics. The copywriters took considerable licence, as few people would have expected Jim to come out with a remark like 'Darn right, son!'*

Left *One of the many trophies Jimmy Clark treasured in his home was the Checkered Flag Award for winning Indianapolis in 1965. The flag was the actual one used at the track when he won the race.*

wedge-shaped Lotus powered by a Pratt and Whitney turbine, and it was this car which Jimmy was going to drive at Indianapolis. Though it is pure conjecture on my part, I can see him fretting his way through the last few days in Australia until he could dash back to Paris and then over to Indianapolis for testing with the bright-crimson turbine. He tried the car out and had obviously enjoyed it when he broke off testing to come back to Europe for the new season and the Formula 2 races at Barcelona and Hockenheim.

Indianapolis was not Jimmy Clark's favourite race, but it kept calling him back, for it was a big adventure and, to Jimmy, that was what motor racing was all about.

Chapter 3

Hockenheim

1968 had all the makings of success for Jim Clark. The Lotus 49 was now a proven chassis, and Clark would be able to make use of the early Tasman series to iron out any further minor development problems before the European season got under way.

Colin Chapman had designed a stunning new Indianapolis car with a wedge-shaped body and a gas turbine engine. It had great potential, and Clark was looking forward to driving the car in early tests at Indianapolis in March of that year. Plans were also afoot to modify the 1967 Lotus 48 Formula 2 car with a different chassis and new suspension location points.

On the financial front the tie-up with Gold Leaf cigarettes promised Jimmy a secure and rewarding season in Formula 1 and Formula 2.

On New Year's Day, Clark was already in action at Kyalami. This, his last Grand Prix race in South Africa, fell into the typical Clark victory pattern for, although Jackie Stewart led on the opening lap, Jimmy stormed past him, holding on to his lead and breaking the lap record in the process. This particular victory called for another entry in the record books, for he had now won 25 Grands Prix and so had become the Grand Prix driver with the record number of wins of all time. During his career, Fangio had won 24 events in the World Championship, and the world had to wait for Jackie Stewart's heyday before Clark's record was broken.

There were many happy days during the early part of 1968, when Clark visited New Zealand and then moved on to Australia. In his eight races 'down under' he chalked up five firsts, one second, one fifth place and a retirement, emerging as the clear winner of the Tasman Championship.

The Hockenheim circuit as it was set up in 1968.

During practice for his last race at Hockenheim Jimmy Clark didn't seem happy with the car and spent a lot of time with chief mechanic Jim Endruweit.

Looking fit and bronzed by the Australian sun, he flew back to Europe to start a new season. Two dates in particular were pencilled into his diary: the Formula 2 race at Barcelona, and the other Formula 2 event at Hockenheim.

Motor racing, like all other sports or pastimes, has its fair share of 'ifs' and 'buts', and in the case of Jim Clark's death it would be fair to say that there was a great deal of controversy about even his actual presence at Hockenheim.

One view was that, on that particular day, he should have been racing for Alan Mann in the Ford sports car at the BOAC race at Brands Hatch, and not in a European F2 event at Hockenheim, which was not his kind of circuit anyway. However, this opinion did not take account of Jimmy Clark's role in the Lotus team. Not only was he on an exclusive driving contract with Lotus, but Lotus had built a team of Lotus 48s to compete in the European Formula 2 Championship for 1968, and the Hockenheim race was the first event counting for that Championship.

There were two Formula 2 races on the calendar before Hockenheim; the

Syracuse event was postponed, so Lotus had to rely on the race at Barcelona, seven days before the European Championship started, for trying out the cars. By a strange quirk of French/Spanish relations, the Barcelona event counted for the French Formula 2 Championship, so Clark broke off his testing of the Indianapolis turbine car to take in both events. He then had a few days testing at Zandvoort marked down in his diary, beginning the day after Hockenheim, and was due to come home to Scotland to see his parents the following weekend.

When he arrived at Barcelona, Jim Clark found a large and impressive entry, including Jackie Stewart in a Matra entered by Matra International, a team run by Ken Tyrrell and John Coombes. Ferrari had brought along two new models based on the V6 Dino engine (the 166) for Chris Amon and Jacky Ickx; these cars were twin-cam 24-valve models with a claimed 225 bhp at 11,000 rpm. Tecno also had a new Formula 2 car driven by Clay Regazzoni, while Brabham had the BT23C, with Jochen Rindt and Alan Rees driving the Winklemann racing cars. Piers Courage, Derek Bell and Chris Lambert were also in Brabhams.

The new alliance of Gold Leaf Team Lotus arrived with cars for Clark and Hill, the latter's being a 1967 model, and Jimmy's an updated type 48. There was another Lotus in the race — the one Clark had used the previous year — driven by Jackie Oliver, who was entered by his local flying club, the Herts and Essex Aero Club.

During practice Jackie Stewart's Matra was quickest with Clark a tenth of a second behind, followed by the Matras of Pescarolo and Beltoise. In the circumstances the old Clark skill was showing, but the wise money was placed on the Matras which were quick and handling well.

The race was a disaster for Jimmy. Stewart jumped into the lead with Clark second and Jochen Rindt and Jackie Ickx crowding behind. Ickx got past Rindt towards the end of the lap and set out hotfoot after Clark. At the hairpin Clark braked in his usual way, only to have the Ferrari collect him heavily, and he found himself spinning backwards down the road with a broken top link in the rear suspension and a broken wheel. Clark was furious about it as he felt Ickx had been stupid to leave his braking so late. What was really concerning him, however, was the knowledge that there was no time for the mechanics to get the car back to the factory before Hockenheim the following Sunday.

A typical pre-Grand Prix season week followed, each day filled with small details to be cleared up. There were also thoughts about Indianapolis, the testing session at Zandvoort, and the Monaco Grand Prix which, no doubt, Clark was determined to win. He spent the Friday evening at a private dinner party, and the next morning was driven out to Toussus-le-Noble airfield outside Paris, where his Piper Twin Commanche was waiting. He had decided to take the aircraft so that he could arrive promptly at Zandvoort for testing on the Monday. Weather conditions that Saturday were not good — there was a threat of snow — but Clark landed safely in Germany.

Hockenheim has had a racing circuit for nearly 35 years. It was in the late 1930s, when Germany was at her peak in Grand Prix racing, that the local authorities around Heidelberg decided to invest in a racing circuit of their own. The area is covered with low hills and woodland, and the circuit itself

Opposite *Jimmy helps to fuel the Formula 2 Lotus in front of the pits at Hockenheim.*

was built near the village of Hockenheim. In its original form it measured 7.72 kms and was roughly oval, with a pair of long, curving straights linked by a wide radius curve at one end and a tight corner at the other. It was obviously planned as a high-speed circuit to demonstrate the Mercedes-Benz and Auto-Union racing cars at their best. The War intervened, however, and, although it was opened in 1939, no major races took part at the circuit for some eight years. Indeed, no lap records seem to have survived from the period, though it is known that Mercedes used the circuit for testing their famous 1.5-litre Tripoli car, the W165.

Although motor racing resumed in France in 1945, it was two years before it started up again in Germany, and Hockenheim was host to one of the first postwar events. The race was won by Hans Stuck, the great pre-war German star, and father of the present Hans Joachim Stuck, in a Cisitalia fitted with a 1,100 cc Fiat engine. When one considers that Stuck averaged nearly 88 mph in a car which was relatively modest in its performance, the real potential of the circuit can be clearly seen. Hockenheim grew very quickly in its popularity so that, by the following year, it was no surprise when more than 200,000 people turned up for a meeting.

However, the circuit fell into disuse in the early 1950s, although Mercedes still occasionally tested their sports and Formula 1 cars there, and, as far as is known, the lap record for the circuit in its original form stands at 128 mph to Stirling Moss and Karl Kling.

During the '50s the National Autobahn programme dictated a route between Heidelberg and Heilbron which would cut the circuit in two, but the local authorities, being well-versed in motorway politics, held out in

The start of heat 1 of the Formula 2 race at Hockenheim. It was a damp, miserable afternoon and already Pescarolo (left) and Beltoise in their Matras had taken the lead from Chris Lambert's Brabham, Piers Courage, Brabham, and then Jim Clark in the centre of the pack in fifth place.

order to obtain the maximum compensation. Early in 1960 the builders had their way, the track closed, and the top was chopped off the egg. The local authorities, meanwhile, went back to their drawing boards and reshaped the circuit with a new grandstand area and a club circuit measuring 2.65 kms. The rest of the circuit retained its original character, with a right-hander after the stands, leading into what was probably the longest right-hand bend of any circuit in the world. Though technically a 'straight', it in fact curved lazily through the trees out to the Grosser Kurs, which is a tighter right-hand bend, and then headed back to the grandstands on another long straight with a very slight left-hand bend. Once the cars came in sight of the grandstands, they turned sharp right up to a tight left-hander, and then through a series of right-hand bends, until they passed the start and finish line. This circuit measured 6.77 kms, and was the one used for the Formula 2 race on April 7 1968.

The entry for the Deutschland Trophy was similar to the gathering at Barcelona the previous week, though Jackie Stewart's Matra was missing. Due to the long haul from Barcelona, all the teams made their way direct to the German circuit and worked on their cars when they arrived. Clark's car was completely rebuilt with new suspension parts, while the Jackie Ickx car was returned to Modena, and Chris Amon brought along a new Dino 166.

A Brands Hatch 500-mile event was being held on the same day, and two notable absentees from Hockenheim were Jackie Ickx, who was driving a Gulf Ford GT40 with Brian Redman, and Jackie Oliver who was to race a Lotus Europa at the Brands meeting.

Matra had the MS7 models for Jean-Pierre Beltoise and Henri Pescarolo, while no less than eight Brabhams were to take part, with Piers Courage, Derek Bell, Picko Troberg, Chris Lambert and Max Mosley among the drivers. Also driving a Brabham was Kurt Ahrens, Junior, who was to be the hero of the day for the local spectators.

There were three short periods of practice on the Saturday, and Clark's problems started when he had to miss the first practice session. This was due to problems with the fuel metering unit, a bug shared by most of the competitors, despite the fact that conditions were windy and dry. It was no surprise to find the two Matras on pole position of the grid with Beltoise 0.7 of a second quicker than his team-mate Pescarolo. The Brabhams were also running well, with Ahrens, Courage and Bell coming next on the grid, followed by Amon and Clark.

During practice Jimmy had been unhappy with his car. He had spun coming into the bowl in front of the stands, and had pitted the car to check the brake balance. He hadn't raced on the track before, but already he said that he hated it: it was difficult to set up a car on a circuit which had a short twiddly bit joined by these long, flat-out straights, and Clark never seemed comfortable at circuits with long straights — a throwback to the early days at Spa. All told, the chemistry was wrong, and Clark was clearly concerned about the race, as contemporary photographs show.

Just to add to Jimmy's discomfiture, he woke up on the morning of race day to see rain on the windows of his hotel room, and it didn't help his mood. When he arrived at the track the rain had begun to ease off, but the road was still soaking wet and the mechanics fitted the car with new wet compound Firestone tyres.

That same morning Colin Chapman set off for a well-deserved holiday to

St Moritz, where he and his family were due to arrive in the early evening.

Eighteen cars started in the first heat and, despite the gloomy scene and slight mist hanging over the track, there was a big crowd in the grandstands. The two Matras flew into the lead from the flag with Kurt Ahrens on their tail, and Clark sneaked through between Amon and Bell to take fifth behind Chris Lambert. In these miserable conditions there was still a lot of sorting out, even on the first lap. Soon it was Beltoise leading from Ahrens, with Bell and Courage, Pescarolo and Irwin, before Clark came through, shadowed by Robin Widdows and Jo Schlesser. At the very back was Walter Habegger in his Valvoline Racing Team Lotus 41. During the course of the next two laps, as the race settled down, Pescarolo restored Matra's hopes by overtaking Bell and Courage, and a lap later the crowd rose to young Kurt Ahrens when he took over the lead from Beltoise. Jimmy, meanwhile, was having a terrible race, dropping back through the field, and Chris Lambert passed him on the fourth lap. Then Habegger crashed his Lotus into the bank near the stands. Within the next few moments the face of motor racing was to change dramatically.

Jimmy was on his own now, with Lambert up ahead of him and Widdows a little way behind. On the fifth lap he left the main stand area, climbing the slight hill out of the bowl and into the woods. At this point the track ran close to the trees; it was a non-spectator area. A lone flag marshal, out where the straight begins to bend slowly, noticed Clark's car twitch one way then the other, before shooting diagonally across the road into some small trees. The car was decimated, the driver dead; the sheer devastation was horrifying.

When the track was rebuilt in the early '60s, some small saplings had been planted at this point, so shielding a steep banking behind which is a small irrigation canal. When the car shot across the road it hit a clump of these saplings which, although quite small, had one tree with a trunk about eight inches in diameter. The impact was exactly at the point where the car's number 1 roundel had been placed, and Jimmy Clark had no earthly chance of survival. Jackie Stewart thought at the time that, if Clark had been wearing full harness, he might have been alive today, but the very impact point was such that there was no way in which he could have avoided death. In that initial impact the engine and rear suspension were torn away from the main monocoque, landing up against the banking about ten yards away. One front wheel was jammed in a vee formed by two branches.

Back at the grandstand few of the spectators were aware of what had happened. Jim Clark had gone missing and then the ambulance went out, but there was no news until the information came back to the pits, and the Lotus pit became a scene of tragedy. Most of the other drivers were oblivious to what had taken place, probably thinking that Clark had retired, dispirited with his lowly eighth position and content not to be out there racing with them. Ahrens retired after a great run, and Jean-Pierre Beltoise won for Matra with Pescarolo in second and Lambert in third place after a spirited drive.

As the drivers slowed they suddenly realised that something tragic had occurred and, as they each trickled to their pit, the air fell silent. Few of them could believe the news; Piers Courage cried openly.

Graham Hill was aware that someone had gone off, but he dared not believe it was Clark, for he knew that there was litle hope for any driver going off the road at a point where speeds were over 140 mph. Hill's car was loaded

During the race Clark ran fairly low in the field and was in eighth place when the accident happened.

away in the transporter, and the mechanics prepared for the task of recovering the remains of Clark's car.

Few drivers had the heart to face a second heat straight away, and there were a couple of races held in the interim. The crowd was still unaware of the tragedy. Eventually it was decided to run the second heat, and 15 cars appeared. Apart from Graham Hill, the only driver to withdraw was Robs Lamplough with his McLaren; he just didn't have the heart to go out and race again. All racing drivers face these decisions in time of tragedy and, wheras the action of the 15 competitors might appear heartless, they knew that nothing would be achieved by abandoning the meeting. Then the spectators were told about Clark's death, and the flags were lowered to half mast. Six hundred miles away at Brands Hatch the crowd was stunned by the news and, a few hundred miles in the opposite direction, the 25,000-strong crowd at the Aspern races near Vienna observed one minute's silence in memory of Clark.

In the final, Beltoise and Pescarolo finished first and second, with Piers Courage in third place; the sad meeting was over.

What caused the accident? There were several theories, and an investigation into the incident was led by Colin Chapman.

Perhaps the most bizarre theory was the one of children on the track. Shortly after the race a man telephoned American motoring journalist Jerry Sloniger, who lived nearby, to tell him that he had photographs of children

running across the track. All that was ever known about the man was that he was a member of the Heidelberg-Mannheim Sports Touring Club: he never produced the film. Nevertheless, local newspapers carried the story that two children had been seen in the vicinity of the accident.

In 1974 I paid a visit to the spot where Jimmy crashed. No spectators are allowed in the area, and the deep woods round about are criss-crossed by paths used by the local foresters. On race days the foresters check out the paths to make sure that no one is wandering around. One theory is that the children might have been known to one of these foresters who gave them permission to nip across the track between the cars. Having seen the spot, I feel that, although it is not impossible that this could have happened, it is highly unlikely. For a start, the track itself is quite wide and it would take about ten or twelve seconds for anyone to run from one side to the other. Then one has to bear in mind the fact that they would have to cross wet, slippery grass on both sides of the track before they could reach cover on the other side. To me it is inconceivable that this could have happened without one of the drivers noticing the incident, and Robin Widdows was not that far behind Clark. Sloniger's own opinion is that, thinking back after the event, the man imagined that he had seen someone on the track, thus giving rise to the whole theory.

Meanwhile, Chapman, oblivious to all that had happened, arrived in St Moritz and booked into his hotel to find a message asking him to telephone Chief Mechanic Jim Endruweit at Hockenheim. Eager to learn the result of the race Chapman made the call, only to be stunned by the news that Clark had been killed. Recalling the moment, Chapman says 'I went into shock. I just couldn't believe it and I jumped into my rental VW and drove off straight for Hockenheim and arrived there in the early hours of the morning.'

He arranged for all the pieces of Clark's car to be carefully gathered together and taken back to the Lotus factory. An official investigation was planned with Colin Chapman, Keith Duckworth of Cosworth, Chris Parry of Firestone and P. F. Jowitt, an RAC scrutineer, whose profession was aircraft accident investigation at Farnborough. The investigation took place on April 11, the Thursday following the accident, and a report was written and sent off to the various interested parties. An abridged version, signed by Colin Chapman, was then released to the press and read as follows:

'Careful examination of every part of the car, including the whole of the front and rear suspension and steering systems, revealed that there was no evidence to indicate that any of these parts had become detached prior to the impact, all retaining bolts were in place, there was no sign of fatigue or failure of any component and each and every fracture of these components was entirely consistent with impact failure and accompanied by deformation of the members themselves, demonstrating that they were performing their correct functions prior to impact.

'The engine and transmission system was dismantled to check for any possible defect which could have caused any unusual condition such as

Opposite *The spot where Jimmy Clark's accident took place photographed in 1974. Since the accident the trees have been cut back and Armco barrier has been put in place. The car probably lost control where the photograph was taken and ended up against the trees marked with an arrow.*

partial or complete seizure but all was found to be in normal condition.

'Only one tyre, the left rear, was still inflated and there was indication of it having slid sideways from right or left over mud and grass. The two front tyres were sound but showed signs of impact and the wheels were fractured. The right rear tyre was deflated and had a small cut in the tread which prevented its retaining air when reinflated.

'Consideration of all these aspects, the reports of a reliable eye witness at the actual scene of the accident, the particular part of the circuit where it occurred, and conditions under which the car would have been operating at the time, make it absolutely impossible to be categoric as to a possible reason for the accident.

'This is corroborated by an extract from the very detailed report made by the RAC scrutineer as follows:

' "Summing up I have come to the following conclusions. Having examined every failed part of the car, most of them under magnification, I can say with no hesitation that there was no evidence whatsoever of pre-impact structural failure. All the failures are entirely consistent with impact damage. The car left the track at very high speed, probably about 120 miles per hour, turning slowly to the right in an oversteering condition, and striking a tree sideways on.

' "It is worth remarking that even so this accident need not have been fatal if adequate crash barriers of the types used at Monaco and elsewhere had been installed to prevent cars which became out of control continuing with almost undiminishing speed into substantial trees lining the roadside." '

There is no doubt in Colin Chapman's mind as to the cause of the accident: it was a puncture of the rear right tyre. At the same time he is convinced that it was such a freak accident that it might only have happened on a circuit like Hockenheim. He reconstructs the accident in the following way.

Jimmy probably picked up something in the tyre on the fourth lap. (In practice the previous day, Walter Habegger had broken the crankshaft of his car, and a small fragment of metal may have been lying in the road.) It didn't need much loss of pressure for the effect to be felt and, when Clark started to go through the twisting piece of track in front of the grandstands, the rear-tyre pressure was possibly down from 15 psi to 10 psi. When he reached one sharp left-hand bend a fellow driver saw him slide and then quickly correct it. As the next corner was a sharp right-hander, the weight of the car would be thrown on to the left-hand side and away from the right rear tyre, and it is assumed that Jimmy put his trouble at the previous bend down to the greasy surface of the track. Even if the pressure had dropped to 8 psi, the tyre would have stayed on the rim as it was a slow right-hand corner. However, once he opened out to the back straight, the steadily rising speed and the steadily deflating tyre brought the power of centrifugal force into play. In tests following the accident it was found that, under these conditions, the tyre would begin to grow and at a crucial point the sidewalls would be drawn in, and there would be an explosive depressurisation as the air rushed out. From that moment an accident was inevitable.

Since then car manufacturers have fitted security bolts to hold the rim to the bead and, looking back at racing conditions at that time, no blame could

Opposite *Marking the place where Jim Clark's Lotus crashed is this small stone cross. In the background is the circuit.*

be attributed to the tyre manufacturers who were, in this case, Firestone. The accident occurred because a series of circumstances fell into place at the same time, with tragic results. It is ironic to consider that Kurt Ahrens, who had sprung into prominence in this race only to fade back into obscurity, claimed that the reason he did so well was that he was running on skinny, out-of-date tyres for the simple reason that he could not afford the more sophisticated ones the experts were using.

At the end of the day, one must accept the analysis of the experts, for want of evidence pointing to any other cause. Certainly few people who know anything about motor racing would credit that the accident was the result of a driving error on Clark's part. At the point where the accident took place Clark would already have been on line for the long open curve and, had a normal tail slide taken place on the greasy surface, he would have smothered it instantly without even thinking. The description of the accident is certainly consistent with something unexpected having occurred. Did some children run out in front of Clark? I find it hardly likely, since not one shred of evidence has been produced to back up this theory.

The effect of the accident on racing and on ordinary people in the street was stunning. I know of a number of racing drivers who went through a period of self-doubt, arguing within themselves that, if a man as brilliant as

Jimmy Clark's body lies buried in the graveyard of the old church at Chirnside which can be seen in the background. Paving stones have been placed around the grave as it is visited by thousands of people from all over the world every year. The black gravestone on the left is that of Willie Campbell the steward, who taught Jimmy all the rudiments of shepherding when he was sixteen.

Clark could get killed, then perhaps there was an inevitability of death in the career of a racing driver. It is therefore encouraging that Jackie Stewart, the man who took over Clark's crown in Grand Prix racing, should go right to the top, surpassing Clark's record number of Grand Prix wins, and then retire, fit and active. Probably, unknown to him, Jackie Stewart has given new self-confidence to an equal number of drivers.

Another result of the accident was that changes were made in the Hockenheimring; two chicanes have been built, one just 50 yards before the point where Jimmy was killed, the other on the return straight. These are rather flat and featureless chicanes, and I wouldn't be surprised if Jimmy would have scorned them. In the same area there is an Armco barrier and a netting fence.

In their methodical way the circuit owners have put a gate in the fence at the point where Jimmy Clark was killed. If ever you should go to the Hockenheim track when there is no race meeting taking place, take the short walk from the stands out into the country. Just beyond the chicane, where the woods stretch to the side of the track, you will find the gate. Step through it and you are among the saplings. There, low on the ground, is the rough stone cross with a collection of wild flowers around it. You will find no manicured lawn, no chains to keep visitors back, just a small cross in virgin soil — the silent memorial to that sad day in April 1968.

Jim Clark's body was brought back to the Borders he knew and loved, and the funeral was arranged for Wednesday, April 10. On that day more than a thousand people made their way to the little village of Chirnside Old Church: a typical Scottish parish church, stone-built, blending with the soft surrounding scenery. It was filled with 600 mourners, and hundreds stood outside in the sunshine, although a chill breeze was blowing, to hear the sermon over the loudspeakers.

Drivers came from all over the world to pay their last respects. They were all there: Graham Hill, Jack Brabham, Jochen Rindt, Jo Siffert, Jo Bonnier, Jackie Stewart, Innes Ireland, Denny Hulme, Dan Gurney, and many more.

The service was conducted jointly by the Reverend Gibson K. Boath and the Reverend J. B. Longmuir, DD, who was later to become Moderator of the Church of Scotland, the highest office in that church. Revd Longmuir was a personal friend of the Clarks, and his sermon was one of the most compassionate and inspired that I have ever heard. It was a simple service beginning with the hymn 'By cool Siloam's shady rill', and ending with the Crimond version of 'The Lord's my Shepherd'. Then everyone filed out to the upper end of the small cemetery where Clark's body was laid to rest. The entire cemetery appeared to be carpeted in flowers, and tributes poured in from all four corners of the globe.

Today the grave is surrounded by paving stones to preserve the area from the thousands of people who annually visit Chirnside church. The marble headstone is one of the largest in the cemetery, and the simple inscription reads 'In Loving Memory of Jim Clark O.B.E. Born 4.3.36 died 7.4.68, Farmer, Edington Mains, Chirnside and of Pembroke Bermuda. World Champion motor racing driver 1963 and 1965, winner of 25 Grand Prix races, Indianapolis 500 winner 1965, First freeman of Burgh of Duns.'

Beside it is another gravestone, that of William Campbell, the steward at Edington Mains, who taught Jimmy Clark so much about farming.

On March 23 1969, many of these old friends went back to Chirnside for the unveiling of the Jim Clark Memorial Clock which was erected in the centre of the village and was paid for by admirers from many countries. It was a quiet, informal gathering and Mrs Clark unveiled the plaque. The clock was designed by Clark's old farming friend, Ian Scott Watson. A local firm built it from stone quarried in the Forest of Dean by well-known motoring commentator, Peter Scott Russell.

Later that same year the Burgh of Duns set aside a room in the Burgh Chambers to house the Jim Clark Trophy Collection which had been given to the Burgh by Jim's family. Duns is on no major road, yet more than 50,000 people have signed the visitors' book and looked round the Trophy Room, of which the Burgh of Duns is justly proud.

It is not only in Scotland that Jim Clark is remembered. There is a Jim Clark Trophy presented in the United States, and he is remembered in Australia and New Zealand; the April meeting at Hockenheim has carried the title, The Jim Clark Memorial Trophy Meeting; and even in Modena, not far from where Ferrari build their racing cars, there is a piece of modern sculpture called the 'Albo della Gloria', erected in Jim Clark's memory. It takes more than just skill on a motor racing circuit to be remembered so.

Chapter 4

What made him tick?

I first became aware of the genus 'racing driver' when I was 16. A new motoring magazine called *Autosport* had just come on the market, costing 6d a copy, and a trumpet-playing friend of my father used to pass his copy on to me. In those days motor racing meant Grand Prix wins by Alfa Romeo and Ferrari, and the efforts of cars like HWM and drivers like Peter Collins and Lance Macklin — not to mention Stirling Moss. At that time I scarcely dreamt that, within seven years, I would be counting such heroes among my acquaintances. In my innocent youth motor racing was a dream world populated by people who were somehow unreal. They walked ten feet tall, they didn't live as mere humans, but as higher beings: nearly every enthusiast has probably gone through the same phase. As time went by and I was able to meet with the drivers, first at the race circuits and then socially, my whole view of them changed. Their cars and their exploits tended to fade and their intrinsic value as people became more important.

One soon realises that there is no archetypal racing driver, and that the next World Champion could be that unemployed guy you see collecting his benefit — as in the case of Graham Hill — or else the cocky little kid down the road with the flash Austin Healey and the jaunty walk to match — like Jackie Stewart. The emergence of a world champion racing driver is not the result of selective breeding, of tender or rich upbringing, or of opportunities served up on a silver plate, but rather the result of a strange chemistry, the ingredients of which exist in nearly all of us, but not in the correct proportions.

In the past 24 years much of my life has been spent either with, or else thinking about, racing drivers, the cars they drive and the people surrounding them. Every time I take another step towards defining their make up another building block in that vast DNA molecule which represents the world champion racing driver is added. I am not alone in this search: others have gone into the subject more deeply. For the past five years I have kept up a spasmodic correspondence with Dr Keith Johnsgard of San José State College in California, who has conducted research into racing driver personality since 1966 and has subjected many drivers to tests and questioning in an attempt to unearth the clues to the make up of this fascinating form of *homo sapiens*.

Johnsgard's work is fascinating, even though many of his conclusions are obvious. He has found that one of the most striking characteristics of the racing driver, as measured by personality tests, is an unusually high need for achievement. The need to be the very best seems to be more dominant in racing drivers than in other sportsmen. Johnsgard found that, even at club level, drivers had set a fairly high achievement hurdle for themselves, with one in eight fledgling drivers determined to be a professional champion.

At the same time the psychologist dismisses the common idea that a racing driver is essentially a person with a strong self-destruction motive. Johnsgard points out that people bent on self-destruction internalise their anger, bury it deep down within themselves, allowing it to erupt to the surface. Sometimes this explosive externalisation of anger takes the form of a terminal act, such as suicide. Racing drivers tend to be the opposite, exposing their anger and frustration after a breakdown perhaps, or being overly demonstrative in an annoying situation. Having studied racing fairly closely, and having read a great deal about the early days, I can find only one occasion when the motor racing circuit was used for suicide. Many novelists have used the theme: Michael Arlen in *Green Hat*; the Earl of Cottenham in his book *Sicilian Circuit;* and, more recently, one of the characters in Nevil Shute's apocalyptic book *On the Beach* goes out and kills himself in his racing car. The lone instance of factual suicide I can find concerned a 30-year-old Czech mechanic called Josef Bradzil, who was killed during practice for the Grand Prix of Czechoslovakia in 1934.

His is a bizarre story, more in keeping with the pages of a novel than with real life. Bradzil arrived at the Czech circuit with a brand-new Grand Prix Maserati; it seems that his fiancée gave the money for the car to his manager. Alas, on the eve of the race, the engagement was broken off and the fiancée issued a summons against both manager and mechanic for the return of the money. The police arrested Bradzil and put him in jail but, after a deputation of drivers had asked that he be released to practice and race, he was

Opposite *Even when wearing gloves Jimmy had a habit of biting his nails.*

Below and pages 92-93 *The many faces of Jimmy Clark: Early in his career Jim Clark could never quite believe that he was capable of winning races, such as here at Aintree.*

Jim Clark Remembered

Left *'When he was worried you could read it all over his face'* — *Sally Stokes.*

Below *All his technical problems were discussed intently with Colin Chapman.*

Bottom *The strain of Grand Prix racing is reflected in Jim Clark's eyes after winning the British Grand Prix in 1965.*

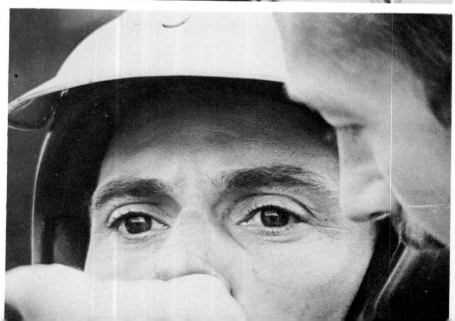

What made him tick?

Right *Occasionally there were moments of doubt, such as here when the engine was not running well at Silverstone during the British Grand Prix meeting.*

Right *Before a race Clark was cool and calm as he checked over all his equipment.*

Below *'When he smiled his whole face lit up' — Sally Stokes.*

set free. Shortly after practice had begun, Bradzil made no attempt to take one of the corners and cannoned into two trees at over 125 mph and was killed instantly. At the inquest it was judged to be suicide while the balance of mind was disturbed.

Nothing in Bradzil's story fits with Johnsgard's psychological graph of the competitive racing driver, but then Bradzil's case was very much an exception.

In a psychological sense then, what constitutes a racing driver?

'He is an individual with an unusually high need to achieve and accomplish tasks that require great skill and effort.

'Coupled with this need to be successful is high endurance and need to work hard at a task until it is completed. The driver is a remarkably aggressive individual with a high need for dominance. He externalises his hostility verbally and will argue for his point of view and attack contrary opinions.

'His need to feel guilt, blame himself, and punish himself is below average.

'He has high leadership capacity and potential but a below average need to join or affiliate with groups and organisations, or to have a large number of close friends. He attains below average scores on intraception, succorance and nurturance which suggest a low need to be needed by other people in emotionally close and sensitive relationships.

'He is a reasonably deferential, orderly and somewhat exhibitionistic man. He is a strongly independent and autonomous individual who would much prefer to do things his own way, and is not basically group-tied or conservative.

'He is an experimenting person with a need for change and extraordinarily tough-minded with a rather tough poise. These traits are asso-

Much of Clark's time was taken up in the lonely task of testing racing cars. Although he occasionally complained about it he still enjoyed finding out as much as he could about the cars he drove.

Clark's sheer enjoyment of racing is perfectly captured in this photograph by his friend Michael Cooper. Despite the wet he is obviously pleased with himself or else is hurling some rude epithet at Cooper as he goes past. If he played up to his photographer friends it was partly because he secretly saw himself as a potentially good motor racing photographer.

ciated with self reliance, no-nonsense, realistic, decisive characteristics as against dependence and sensitivity.

'Contrary to the common public image the driver is a reserved, somewhat detached, critical and cool individual. He is an emotionally stable individual who faces reality and has low scores on neuroticism.' (*The Competition Racing Driver* — A preliminary report, by Keith W. Johnsgard, PhD, and Bruce C. Ogilvie, PhD, published by the Journal of Sports Medicine and Physical Fitness, USA.)

During Johnsgard's studies in California in the late 1960s and early 1970s he asked one particular question of novice drivers: 'Which of the world's racing drivers (living or dead) would you most like to drive like?' One name occurred more frequently than any other: Jim Clark.

Why is it that, years after his death, motor racing enthusiasts around the world still revere the name of Jim Clark? Why is it that 1974 Indianapolis winner Johnny Rutherford, on receiving the Jim Clark Memorial Trophy in the United States some time ago, said 'I know now that I think about him so much and only wish that I could better emulate his example in every way'. Why is it that, when Russian cosmonaut Yuri Gagarin shook hands with Clark, he said 'I suppose you'll be as proud of me as I am of you'?

Jim Clark represented for many people everything that is good about motor racing, and what one would call the 'good life'. He was polite, he was modest, he was kind-hearted, and calm to the point of wandering almost as if in a dream through the motor racing scene. Yet he was so talented as a driver, and that talent shone through to even the least interested spectator.

I often wonder why it is that we always wish to compare people's performances. For instance, most people I have spoken to have wanted to compare Clark with the other supermen of racing, men like Louis Renault, Tazio Nuvolari, Berndt Rosemeyer, Juan Fangio, Stirling Moss and Jackie Stewart. How can one compare their performances? I feel that a driver like Louis Renault was a real superman among supermen when you consider that he won his races at the turn of the century in a car weighing nearly two tons, with braking efficiencies less powerful than that of the hand brake of a modern car, and on roads with no billiard-table surface, but populated by such unpredictable things as dogs, cats, hens and people. In those circumstances, to average more than 60 mph from Paris to Bordeaux is a motor racing feat which the rest would find difficult, if not impossible, to equal.

The truth is that — just as it is impossible to say with any conviction that Renaissance painting is better than Post-Impressionist — so you cannot honestly cross-refer between drivers of different eras in motor racing: each represents the best of an age. There is no doubt that Jim Clark was the best from 1961 until his death, and might have remained so for another two or three years, by which time he would certainly have retired and left the stage to his great friend Jackie Stewart. By his death we lost out on what would have been some tremendous battles between Clark and Stewart, just as we lost out at the beginning of Clark's Grand Prix career when Stirling Moss had his severe accident at Goodwood in 1961. Both Clark and Moss bitterly regretted that they could not have raced against each other more often in equal cars. Indeed, Clark's reverence for Moss' ability was similar to Stewart's for Clark. Regrettably, too, Clark never raced against Juan Fangio and, to my knowledge, he never even saw Fangio race, but it was Fangio who came back in 1965 and remarked at Monza that, in his opinion, Clark was the greatest racing driver in the world.

The more one looks into Jim Clark's life the more one realises that he was a very ordinary human being who had the good fortune to discover his true vocation in life, as opposed to the many millions who have never realised their own potential. Once given the opportunity, he was quick to appreciate his own ability, and he was one of the few racing drivers I have known with a superiority complex when it came to driving. It is true that he would constantly display outward signs of self-doubt, but in the crucial moments he made his own decisions and went ahead.

It is now almost 20 years since I first met Clark, and at that time he was involved in motor sport in a very low-profile way. He ran his Sunbeam Mark III in driving tests and the odd rally and always seemed to be fast and neat; well, almost always. Normally he was notable for being very tidy on the road with no histrionics. He was essentially a motoring enthusiast whose interest could be sparked off by almost any aspect of motoring.

Back home on the farm Jimmy took his duties to heart and spent most of the time either out in the fields with the sheep or else filling in forms for farm grants. Here he inspects one of his lambs.

In those early years his involvement in motor racing was comparable in its intensity to that of a horse racing enthusiast. Whenever he was in Edinburgh he would call in at the house to catch up on all the latest motoring magazines. He had a particularly zany sense of humour and was a great fan of American motoring writers Stan Mott and Henry Manney who managed to make motor racing both interesting and amusing.

Much has already been written about the key points in his career — the first race meeting, the arrival of the D-type Jaguar, etc — but throughout this period Jim Clark was a farmer who spent most of his time wrestling with the accounts and cursing the government over subsidies. To him the Kelso Ram Sales were more important than Silverstone, and it has often been said that his rural upbringing gave him something solid to fall back on, and an attitude towards life which allowed him to put his subsequent motor racing career into the correct perspective. He never failed to be amazed at the most ordinary things, and went through life with a wide-eyed fascination for almost everything around him.

Early in his career Clark was convinced that a racing driver should be thrown into the deep end as soon as possible so that he can prove to himself that he can race competitively. Certainly, when Border Reivers first purchased the D-type Jaguar for Clark to drive — his previous racing experience being no greater than driving a perfectly standard Porsche 1600 Super — he took to it like a duck to water, and at a testing session at Charterhall, the local Scottish circuit, he was soon lapping competitively. His friend and mentor, Ian Scott Watson, on the other hand, was almost reduced to tears because, on that same day, he realised that he would never become a big-time racing driver as, due to his poor eyesight, his speed of reaction was just not up to sharing the driving of the D-type. So it was a fellow farmer and Border Reiver, Jimmy Somervail, who drove the car with Clark that year. Sadly, Jimmy Somervail, who had raced cars like Lotus 11s and Formula 2 Coopers, retired from racing at the end of that season, partly because he felt that he couldn't match Clark's brilliant driving.

It is interesting to note here that Ian Scott Watson in later years was, like Clark, to give up farming for his true vocation in life as a natural-born architect, and he was one of the founders of Celtic Homes, the timber-frame house manufacturers.

Perhaps the most enigmatic area of Clark's life centred round his relationships with people. To some he appeared shy when, in fact, a better description would have been 'reserved'. I cannot remember my impressions on meeting him for the first time, but then these impressions would matter little, as I first met Clark at a very low level of motor sport where racing was pure fun, and neither of us wanted anything from the other. In later years he became much more wary, which was a great pity in many respects.

His enthusiasm for life bubbled over, and his friends were mainly local farmers with whom he shared such activities as local hops, run by the Young Farmers' Club. When he came into motor sport he enjoyed the weekend rallies where he would navigate for one of his friends or else compete in his

The road car Jimmy Clark used in the early '60s was a Lotus Elan in which he used to make rapid trips northwards to his farm.

It didn't matter whether he was driving flat out down the straight at Aintree or Silverstone, Jimmy Clark was prone to give his photographer friends two-finger vilification; but if he was leading a race by a large margin, he would make signals to photographers moving them into the right position, and then deliberately set the car up in a lurid position so that they could get a good picture.

favourite event, the Border Rally, run on special stages over private roads, long before forestry special stages came along.

To his friends Clark was very open about life and his racing, but his relative innocence when he first started must have led to a number of disappointments in the harsh reality of big-time racing. Because of these disappointments he lost much of this open attitude. In fact, Jackie Stewart admits that it was only a long time after they started to share a flat in London that Clark would take him into his confidence.

Jimmy hated hangers-on and, although he would keep a smile on his face when they were around him, you could tell by his eyes that he was thinking about something else. I remember on one occasion, at the 1964 British Grand Prix, spending the whole of Thursday and Friday practice, as well as race day, wandering around the pits at Brands Hatch without once talking to Jimmy, although I had seen him often. As a result of this I received a telephone call on the Monday and the voice at the other end asked 'What the hell was wrong with you last week?' I explained to him that every time I went to talk to him there was a ring of people around him, and I didn't want to get in the way. 'Och, don't worry about that, they were just wasting time,' he remarked.

In the last years of his life he was visibly opening out more and had learned to be much more relaxed with people he might previously have thought of as his social superiors. Essentially, however, he had achieved this by continuing to be himself, not putting on airs and graces. When he saw that people respected him for it he visibly relaxed.

The basic honesty in his make up was not to be trifled with, and let anyone beware who tried to take advantage of Clark whether in business or in a personal relationship. Indeed, this led to his undoing on some occasions, no more so than in his relationship with fellow Scot Innes Ireland. For the last six years of his life Jim Clark had a personal feud with Innes, and both of them were guilty of the stubbornness which is characteristic of many Scots.

Of all the Grand Prix drivers of the early 1960s Innes knew Jimmy better than any. For a start his background was similar to Jimmy's in that his father was a Ministry of Agriculture veterinary surgeon in the Scottish Borders and knew the Clark family well. Mr Ireland would visit the Clarks and in turn, when Innes became fascinated by motor racing, he had a friend in Alec Calder, another Border farmer married to Jim Clark's eldest sister Mattie. Alec had been racing a Brooklands Riley with great success, and occasionally his teenage brother-in-law had seen him race at Charterhall. When Alec decided to retire from racing he sold the Riley to Innes Ireland who started out on his racing career with that very car. It was a number of years before Jim Clark started racing, by which time Innes was driving for Écurie Ecosse and Lotus. They eventually joined forces in 1960 as team-mates with Team Lotus, who made history that year at the French Grand Prix when they fielded a three-car Grand Prix team composed entirely of Scotsmen, the third driver being Ron Flockhart.

Ireland and Clark got on well together, as Jimmy needed a friend in the big world of motor racing and Innes, another very patriotic Scot, was pleased to have a countryman alongside him. As time went by, however, Clark's ability began to show, and by the end of the 1961 season they were running as equals. At the US Grand Prix, the last event of the season, Innes Ireland gave Colin Chapman his first Grand Prix win under the Team Lotus banner (Stirling Moss had already won for Lotus, but in Rob Walker's independent car). From that moment the relationship between Innes and Jimmy began to break down.

Shortly after the race, Innes went to Paris to race an Aston Martin in the Prix de Montlhéry for GT cars. When he returned he met Geoff Murdoch. the competitions manager of Esso, who were heavy backers of Lotus, and asked about plans for the 1962 season. Murdoch referred him to Colin Chapman. To Ireland's surprise he was told that his services were no longer required and then, as if to add insult to injury, Innes found out that Trevor Taylor was going to South Africa to race for Lotus.

Remembering these times today, Innes admits that he took the whole affair badly and felt that Jimmy had had something to do with his dismissal. Essentially a romantic, Ireland found that the fun had gone out of racing, and he was faced with the big bad world of wheeling and dealing. To make matters worse, he then accepted a deal to drive for UDT in Formula 1, and 24 hours later was offered a works drive for BRM which he felt he had to

On other occasions, such as here at the British Grand Prix at Silverstone, he would fix the photographer with a stare, as though posing to have his picture taken.

turn down, having already given his word to drive for UDT. It is also ironic that, at about the same time, both Ireland and Clark had been approached by Ferrari and, recalling this today, Ireland sagely remarks 'I wish we had both gone'.

What happened next was predictable. Ireland began grousing about Clark, and Clark — who to the day he died insisted that he had no part in Ireland's sacking — felt that if Innes was going to be so shirty about it all, well, he'd be shirty back.

Indeed, it got so bad that Clark once told me he thought Ireland had tried to force him off the track at Monza, but Ireland countered by saying that he (Ireland) was in front and ' . . .bugger him, if he wants to get past he can get past, but I'm not getting out of his way'. Clark, who was actually lapping Ireland at the time, was equally adamant that Ireland should get out of his way.

So it went on. They rarely spoke to each other, yet the animosity was burning up both of them inside. Reflecting on it last year, Ireland said 'The one thing I am desperately sorry about, and one of the ghastly finalities about death is that I'll never be able to make my peace with Jimmy; and you know it's an awfully difficult thing to live with.

'I allowed the same feeling to affect my relationship with Trevor Taylor when he went to South Africa in my place. The whole thing was such an intense personal wound. I hadn't been a naughty boy and I took a lot of it out on Trevor which was quite absurd. I realised it eventually and I made my peace with Trevor and apologised to him, but I never did with Jimmy.'

It is significant that, at the time of the accident, Innes was Sports Editor of *Autocar,* and was covering the BOAC Trophy race at Brands Hatch when Clark's death was announced. He went back home that night and wrote one of the most moving obituaries written by anyone involved in the sport, and to most people who knew of the feud which had existed between Innes and Jimmy, that obituary made his peace.

Chapter 5

The heart and the family

Two years after Jimmy Clark was killed a South African astrologer sent his mother an astrological chart and description of Clark's make up and, although society is sceptical of such matters, some of the statements ring very true. From the pages and pages of data and diagrams there emerges a picture of Jimmy Clark which contains as many intangibles as Jimmy himself displayed in life. I have no idea whether Jimmy ever met this astrologer, but I tend to think that he didn't, in which case the accuracy of his assessment of Jimmy's personality is remarkable.

Under the heading of personality one finds the statement 'Jim Clark was a very proud person, and one might say that the question of pride played a very important part in any relationships or activities throughout his lifetime. However, I'm sure that anybody who did not know him very well (casual acquaintances) would form the opinion that he was not an emotional or sensitive person at all. Jim Clark tended to keep his whole personality completely in the background. This can be seen by the position of the moon in the 12th house (confinements). In this case confinement of personality, also a distinct like of seclusion and a dislike for publicity.'

The horoscope went on to refer to Jimmy's close links with his mother, and the fact that he was likely to experience disappointment, disillusionment and frustration in love affairs generally.

Jimmy was born at 3.20 pm on March 4 1936 at Kilmany in Fife, where his parents farmed, and six years later the family moved to the Borders where they have remained.

Jim Clark, second from the right, in an unsophisticated pose at a race meeting, still wearing his farmer's 'bib' over-alls. On this occasion he wasn't competing, and it was to be another year before he raced a motor car of any kind. His friend and mentor Ian Scott Watson has his back to the camera.

The solid stonework of Edington Mains farmhouse. This typical border farmhouse was built to withstand the cold winds of winter and had walls nearly two feet thick. It also contained a ghost, the Grey Lady, and Jimmy Clark claimed to have seen her when he was very young.

Perhaps the most rewarding part of Jimmy's youth was having four sisters all older than himself; this seemed to make for a very close and happy family life. Jimmy's schooling included a private prep school followed by Loretto, one of Scotland's leading public schools, and one which tends to be favoured by the farming community. Perhaps it was because of this early exile that Jimmy always looked forward to going home and back to the family.

His four sisters are all married, the oldest, Martha (Mattie), being married to Alec Calder, another Border farmer who, it could be said, first brought motor racing into the family. Alec raced a Brooklands Riley in the early 1950s when motor racing first came to Scotland and, occasionally, Jimmy would go along to watch. Mattie and Alec have three children. His sister Susan, who is a BSc, MRCVS, and a lecturer at Edinburgh's Dick Veterinary College, is also married to a farmer, former Scottish rugby international Ken Smith, and they have one child. The third sister is Isobel who is married to Douglas Henderson, a grain merchant from Edinburgh, and they have two children. The youngest of the four sisters is Betty, married to Donald Peddie who farms at nearby Ednam, and they also have two children.

One of Jimmy's great delights was collecting watches which he kept in a drawer at home in Edington Mains. Successful racing drivers always seemed to be presented with watches of all shapes and sizes. When I asked him about his collection, he said, 'I'm trying to build up the numbers until I have one for each of my nephews'. There is still a link with motor racing in the family as Jimmy's cousin, Douglas Niven, is one of the most successful saloon car drivers in Scotland.

When Jimmy Clark grew up and came of age to sit the driving test he passed easily, but his motoring was restricted to mundane saloon cars; not for him the flashy sports car. He left school at 16 and went straight back to the farm where his father wasted no time in getting Jimmy out in the fields earning his keep. 'He bought me a dog and gave me a stick and told me to get

on with it' recalled Clark later, and in those early days he learned much from
Willie Campbell, the farm steward. Indeed, so much did he learn that, two
years later, Jimmy's father suggested that he take over Edington Mains farm
which is just off the main road between Chirnside and Berwick-upon-
Tweed. The land stretched down to the old mill by the River Whiteadder, a
geographical feature which came in useful once when Colin Chapman flew
up to see Jimmy. Colin's instructions consisted of flying to Berwick-upon-
Tweed and turning westwards, following the course of the river until he saw
the red barns of Edington Mains farm!

When he started to race Jimmy realised that his mother would not
approve, so he mentioned it to his father instead: 'I'm having a go at motor
racing, but don't tell Mum.' However, he couldn't keep this new interest to
himself for long and, one day, when running his mother to the farm, he
casually told her that he was going to take up motor racing seriously. 'I told
him "Jim, you are doing nothing of the kind",' said Mrs Clark, 'but he just
flicked the steering wheel back and forward, swerving the car from side to
side to show me that he knew what he was doing.'

Left *A local blacksmith produced this ornamental farm
sign for Jim Clark, and the sign
still stands on the Chirnside to
Berwick-upon-Tweed road.*

Below *In the 1955 International Scottish Rally Jimmy
Clark appeared as navigator
for fellow Border farmer Billy
Potts in this Austin Healey
100. Here they await the start
of a driving test at Ganavan
Sands near Oban. It was in this
car on this rally that Jimmy
first drove at over 100 mph.*

Mrs Helen Clark is a wonderfully attractive woman who is much at home with her eight grandchildren and is both warm-hearted and hospitable. She can talk about Jimmy's racing today, although up till recently the memory was too painful. Jimmy's father is also remarkably fit, although he has suffered various illnesses through the years, illnesses which caused Jimmy a great deal of concern. Mr Clark was always justifiably proud of his son's success in motor racing, and after Jimmy was killed he travelled to Hockenheim in 1969 to present the Jim Clark Memorial Trophy personally.

For them both Jim's death was a great shock. That Sunday afternoon Mr Clark had been watching his favourite farming programme on television and, once it was over, he switched the set off, missing the news flash which was broadcast shortly afterwards. The Clarks' telephone was out of order, so no one could get in touch with them. Ignorant of what had happened, they both set out to visit a friend who had recently been to Bermuda and wanted to show them her colour slides. Alas, this friend heard the news first and, though she knew the Clarks, she didn't feel that she knew them well enough to be the one to break the news, so she got in touch with one of Mrs Clark's

Above *Jim Clark's hands on the wheel of his Lotus Elan. Although he had relatively thin wrists he had strong fingers and forearms. His thumb nail shows the ravages of persistent nail biting.*

Above right *Jim Clark's mother, Mrs Helen Clark, photographed at her home. Mr and Mrs Clark now live in a new house in the grounds of Edington Mains Farm where Jim lived.*

Right *Though outwardly relaxed at home in Edington Mains, Jim would still nervously claw at his finger nails.*

oldest friends who was waiting to tell the Clarks when they arrived. Jimmy's sister Susan and her husband Ken drove Mr and Mrs Clark back to their own house where they were met by Mattie and her husband Alec.

Jimmy Clark inherited many of his finest attributes from his mother and today Mrs Clark can look back on Jimmy's racing and say 'I didn't approve of it, but when he did so well I was really proud of him, but it gave me a lot of worry. After the accident I thought my worries were really over and I could watch motor racing. I never saw him race and even now I'm glad I didn't. I asked Jim to give it up a number of times, but he told me he might as well be killed enjoying himself than die in his bed.'

Today Mr and Mrs Clark live in a new house in the grounds surrounding Edington Mains and are never lonely. All the photographs and souvenirs given to Jimmy during his racing career are preserved, as are all his letters home. Mr and Mrs Clark last saw Jimmy in Bermuda before he flew to Australia, and their last letter from him told them that he would be visiting

Every sideboard and mantelpiece in his house contained trophies of some kind, including this motley collection. In the centre is the magnificent Esso Trophy presented to Jimmy in recognition of all his successes. It is a golden helmet encrusted with rubies.

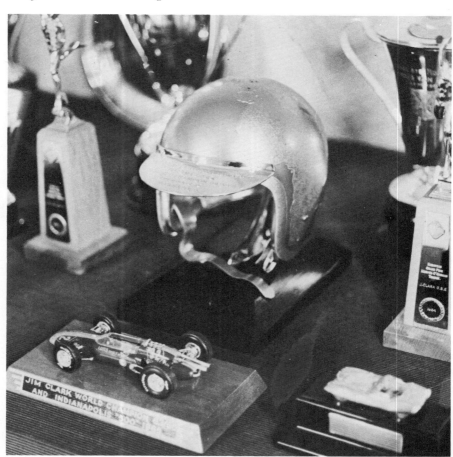

them around April 14 1968. He didn't live to keep that appointment.

To this day letters and cards arrive from close friends and fans of Jimmy, and one telegram which Mrs Clark treasures arrived on their doorstep one year after the Hockenheim accident. It reads:

'A year has passed and my thoughts are with Jimmy as so often during the past season. I miss him very much at all the circuits and I ask you please to accept my sincere feelings of sympathy in these sad days of April. Sincerely, Dan Gurney.'

If there was one thing which Jimmy would not discuss publicly it was personal matters such as girl-friends, and he maintained this reticence to the end of his life. He was determined that he would not get married while he still raced and this led to its own problems, because he reached a stage where he wanted to get married but also loved his racing and didn't want to give it up. The great irony is that, just one week before his death, he confided in Colin Chapman that he was seriously thinking of settling down and getting married.

Part of the reason for Jimmy's silence about his love life was his shyness and self-consciousness when it came to women, which some might agree is almost a characteristic trait of middle-class Scots. In the very early days he viewed the female camp followers of motor racing with wide-eyed innocence. A typical anecdote tells of his conversation with Jabby Crombac at Le Mans. Jabby could always be counted on to bring along some stunning girl to the races, and on this occasion an admiring Jimmy pulled him to one side and asked him how it was that he could pick up girls like that.

However, he did have a string of girl-friends, the most important one being Sally Stokes. Sally first saw Jim race at Mallory Park when he had the Lister Jaguar, but it was 1963 before she met him in person, thanks to some conniving by racing driver John Whitmore and his wife Gunilla.

It was June 1963 and Clark had just finished in second place at Indianapolis and was racing at Crystal Palace. The two were introduced and then didn't meet for another two months. It seemed obvious that Gunilla Whitmore was out to make something of this encounter, as it was she who invited Sally to lunch one day, a day when Jimmy was also there for lunch. Then Gunilla excused herself, saying she had to get some pictures taken, and left the two of them to do the washing up.

Gunilla was later to admit that it was all a put-up job by Jimmy, as he hadn't taken Sally's telephone number the first time they met and was eager to see her again. Their first date was the premier of the epic film 'Cleopatra'.

At that time Sally was modelling for the Jean Bell agency in London, having moved to the city from Wolverhampton where she was brought up. She was in demand for advertising photography rather than as a fashion model as she is small in stature; car companies used her, as her comparatively diminutive size tended to make the cars appear bigger than they actually were.

Sally and Jimmy went about together for more than three years and, though Jimmy was to have many girl-friends in the latter part of his life, Sally somehow always seemed to be the right person for him.

Recalling their relationship, however, Sally is quick to point out that both were Pisceans — their birthdays were only a week apart — and all Pisceans are difficult to get on with. As a result, each could recognise the other's faults only too well.

The heart and the family

Jimmy Clark's longtime girl-friend Sally Stokes expresses both the tension and elation of motor racing. Sally married Dutch racing driver Ed Swart in 1967.

The fact that Jim Clark said he would never get married while he was racing was an indication that it was perhaps the responsibility of marriage which bothered him, and on more than one occasion he asked Sally whether he should give up racing. She was wise enough to realise that, had she made the decision for him, she would have had to live with it for the rest of her life. This odd and ironic trait of Jimmy's — almost preferring other people to make some of his decisions for him — was very touching in some respects, and reflected his honest and earnest approach to life and the people he knew and liked. As a generalisation it could be said that he had many acquaintances but few friends, for he took a long time to get to know people properly and, even after he had known them many years, he would still come out with remarks or actions which seemed out of character.

With girls he was polite and hospitable and, although in the early years he was shy, later he was to take much more advantage of the opportunities which arose for him in the way of girl-friends, opportunities which came about simply because of the prominent role he played in society as the world's number one racing driver.

Though he truly believed that marriage and racing didn't mix, as far as the press were concerned he was aware that it was a good excuse for getting

Left *A cheerful Jimmy Clark at a Dorchester cocktail party with Sally Stokes.*

Below *Occasionally Jim was persuaded to do some advertising pictures for Ford Motor Company, in this case for the Ford Corsair. Occupying the foreground, however, is top model Jean Shrimpton and, for once, Jim Clark had to take a back seat.*

newspapermen off his back. As he said 'It's the easiest way to keep them quiet, isn't it?'

He was never a fashion plate before he was involved in serious motor racing — his taste in clothes being very 'Border farmer' with autumn-tinted tweeds and flat hats — and Gunilla Whitmore and her friend Isobel Pearce were responsible for getting him out of the shapeless bags he used to wear and into smarter clothes bought from some of the better tailors. He grew to like this and became very fussy about his appearance. I remember his pained expression when he described the clothes he had to select when he collected a multi-thousand-dollar wardrobe from a men's store in Indianapolis after he won the race in 1965. The thing which hurt most of all was the fact that he had to choose a whole lot of ties and just couldn't find any that he really liked, so he was forced to take some which he later gave away.

As for his views on the clothes his girl-friends should wear, he was equally adamant. Once, when Sally was obviously fishing for compliments, he remarked 'If it's all right you won't hear any comment from me, I'll only say anything if it isn't all right'.

Of all the memories Sally has of Jimmy Clark, his droll and dry sense of humour is probably the most lasting. It is said that Scots have a macabre sense of humour and tend to have mixed values. Perhaps some of the essentially humorous approach Jimmy Clark had to life is revealed in a letter he sent Sally on March 3 1964, the day before his birthday. Sally was in Switzerland at the time. The letter is typically brief and to the point:

'Dear Sally,

'Just a hurried note to thank you for your letter and say that I will be at Gatwick on the 9th to meet you. Eventually arrived here [*London*] last night after a few hectic days rushing about from the British skating champion-ships on Saturday night in Ayr to running out of lights at night and getting stuck in Doncaster and to rolling a racing Cortina at Goodwood yesterday

Back home on the farm Jim Clark liked nothing better than to change into an old sports jacket and flannels and relax. Here he makes fun of the size of Colin Chapman's Ford Galaxie.

avoiding hitting Colin [*Chapman*] who was spinning in another one. I'll tell you more about that on Saturday.

'Cheers for now, with much love

'Jim.'

By 1966 Sally and Jimmy were seeing less of each other. They had been going about together for over three years and, on one occasion when Jim was abroad, she met Eddy Swart on a blind date in London arranged by Warwick Banks. Eddy was in Britain to race and he knew Warwick who drove Mini-Coopers at that time. Little did Warwick know that Eddy and Sally were to see a lot more of each other, and that nine months before Jim Clark's death they were to marry and live in The Hague.

Although Sally was his constant companion for more than three years, Jimmy had many girl-friends whose company he obviously enjoyed. Though he outwardly never appeared to take girls seriously, underneath he thought deeply about the problems involved, and he occasionally sought out the happily married Helen Stewart for her advice.

As time went on Jimmy was seen with some of the most beautiful girls who hung about the periphery of racing, and he ultimately became a regular man-about-town, no matter where he raced. But to the end his innate self-control made sure that his personal feelings would not interfere with his racing, as he knew it could endanger his life. His solid and secure family background had taught him a lot of good sense.

Right *One of Jim Clark's strangest races took place at the Ingliston circuit near Edinburgh when, at a meeting sponsored by the Milk Marketing Board, a number of drivers was invited to cover one lap in electric milk floats, stopping to pick up milk bottles on the way. Here Jim accelerates on his way to a collection. He didn't win.*

Opposite *On occasions Jim Clark was not seen at his sartorial best, such as here at Oulton Park where he self-consciously posed for this picture wearing a much-stretched cardigan over his racing overalls. He claimed that the weather was cold.*

Below *Jim Clark and girl-friend Sally Stokes at the pits for a sports car race at Oulton Park. Sally was his regular timekeeper and lap scorer.*

Chapter 6

Friends and admirers

Even if Jimmy occasionally fell out with his friends, in the main they were very loyal to him and he to them.

In the last few years Jimmy had a great friend and admirer in Jackie Stewart; Jackie owed a lot to Jimmy in the early days and he admits that Clark taught him many things about motor racing. Perhaps Jackie outstripped Jimmy in terms of business but, even if he was slow at the start, Jimmy soon realised his own potential acumen when he saw what Jackie was worth and, just as Jimmy had taught Jackie a few rudimentary tricks of the racing business, so in turn Jackie taught Jimmy a few of the tricks involved in capitalising on success as a racing driver.

Jimmy Clark's death came as a great shock to Jackie Stewart. That Sunday afternoon Jackie was at the Jarama racing circuit in Spain, doing a track inspection on behalf of the Grand Prix Drivers' Association. As the leading spokesman on track safety at the time, Jackie took his role seriously. He was steadily walking his way round the track, inspecting kerbing on one side and safety fencing and barriers on the other. Little did he know that, at the same moment as he was looking at the steel Armco fencing at Jarama, his friend Jimmy Clark was killed at Hockenheim, perhaps for the lack of it.

Jackie was about half way round the circuit when a car dashed up and a Spaniard told him that Jimmy Clark had been killed. When asked where, the Spaniard said 'Hockenheim'. Jackie replied that he must have made a mistake as Jimmy was surely racing at Brands Hatch. Nevertheless, Jackie cancelled the rest of the inspection on the spot and headed back to Madrid to check. The car broke down, and it was much later, in a restaurant, before he was able to telephone Helen and have the grim news confirmed. That night on Spanish television he was interviewed, and as it came to the end the interviewer said to him 'You now take the crown of motor racing'.

'It was the beginning of a very confusing period for me,' said Stewart. 'I had just left Britain to live abroad so my emotions at that time were very mixed, and it was only later in the season at the American Grand Prix that I remember thinking positively that I had driven a race that Jimmy would have been proud of. It was the first time I was physically and mentally conscious of being able to control the pace and understand what Jimmy must have felt like when he drove. It was as if I had entered a new era and it was a new experience. I felt I had won the race as I had wanted, not because I had any special advantage over everybody else, but because they were prepared to come second to me.'

Opposite *One of Jim Clark's closest racing friends was Jackie Stewart, and it was Clark who persuaded Colin Chapman during practice for the 1964 British Grand Prix to let Stewart try out the Formula 1 Lotus at Brands Hatch. Clark gives his friend instructions.*

An embarrassing moment for Clark came at the Aintree 200 race early in the 1960s, when his Lotus stalled on the line. As the flag comes down Clark looks anxiously over his shoulder and stretches his hand up, while Graham Hill lines up to go past and team-mate Trevor Taylor tries to get round him.

I asked Jackie what he would preserve in his mind as the essence of Jim Clark.

'I'd just like everybody to have the benefit of having spent time with him as we spent time with him. He had a total inability to make any decisions and he was a very innocent individual, and although the pressure of today's racing is something Jimmy never experienced — and even though he had many commitments at the time he died, they were a fraction of what I have gone through — I think, however, he would have adapted to modern sponsorship, because in the last year of his life he was the most complete Jimmy I ever saw. It would have been a battle for him to adjust, but I think he would have met the challenge, for he was beginning to speak very well and very confidently, something he could never do before, and he found he could handle himself more easily in interviews on television.'

As for Jimmy's racing exploits, many of his races will be remembered wherever racing enthusiasts meet. To Colin Chapman, the man closest to Jimmy Clark in his racing, one race stands out: the Italian Grand Prix at Monza in 1967.

The Monza race took place at a time when Lotus and Firestone were trying to develop tubeless tyres and were running tubeless tyres with tubes in them — a kind of belt and braces operation. However, for some unknown reason, the tube in one of Jimmy's tyres lost all its air, started to gather up inside the tyre and twisted over to one side, putting the tyre out of balance. Jimmy came rushing into the pits for a new wheel and tyre.

Ordinarily this would have marked the end of any challenge for the lead,

Television was always a bit of a chore for Jimmy Clark, particularly when the crews came to his farm. Here a BBC Scotland film crew with producer Jock Mearns prepare a programme on Clark's 1963 World Championship with a background of the outbuildings at the farm. Clark is holding his favourite shepherd's crook.

as at Monza part of the game is to stay in the slipstream of your competitors and take every last fraction of advantage. Also, in any Grand Prix, it is unthinkable to contemplate coming into the pits for a wheel change and then going out again with a hope of winning.

Jimmy stormed out of the pits a lap behind and not only caught the leaders to unlap himself, but managed to get so far ahead that the leaders couldn't hold on to his tow, and so he made up an entire lap on them to repass them and take the lead once more: truly an outstanding performance. Sadly, the power he had used in performing this feat meant that he ran out of petrol on the last lap. Despite the demoralising disappointment of it all, Jimmy walked back to the pits and said calmly to Chapman 'You know, Colin, I wish you had put enough petrol in the car' and just walked away. Recalling the incident Colin Chapman remarks 'It's the only time he ever mentioned the matter of running out of petrol, he didn't nag, he didn't moan, it was unbelievable and I've never had a driver like him. He sliced me down to size with just one little remark like that.'

When the car was inspected after the race it was found that there was plenty of fuel in it. The team had been experimenting with safety foam in the fuel tanks to stop the liquid sloshing about, but they had overlooked the fact that it was a degree of fuel surge which helped to keep the catch-tank full when the car was running low on fuel. Whereas, in the normal way, the car would have run out of fuel with only half a gallon of petrol left in the tank, Jimmy's car in that race had nearly 2½ gallons of fuel left when the flow stopped, as the foam had prevented the petrol from filling the catch-tank.

Jackie Stewart also recalled that race. 'I think Jimmy went back and drove his heart out not because he was going to win, but because he was determined to drive the best race that Jim Clark could. And it's fun, you know, when you come out of the Ascari curve at Monza and see the rear wheels of the car in front disappear round the Parabolica, and the next time you come round you see the whole car, and then you see it going into the corner, and all the time you are catching it. It is easy for me to imagine Jimmy in that race sizing up everyone, noticing the man he is catching getting ragged as he sees you creeping up, and taking advantage of his raggedness to smoothly pick up another few yards. Having done a similar sort of thing in my last Italian Grand Prix in 1973 I think I know the elation Jimmy must have felt in that position of being the underdog, with very little to lose and everything to gain. You seem to rise above yourself and it's a great feeling.'

'Jimmy had a fantastic intelligence, he was so quick,' says Colin Chapman. 'I don't think I've ever had dealings with anyone in my life before or since who could pick things up so quickly. You only had to tell him something once and not only did he understand, but he could extrapolate and go beyond the point you had made. During our relationship we built up our own language, so that we could understand each other and I could tell by innuendo what was going on in the car. He never used to exaggerate, so it was easy to tell whether something was serious or not by the degree of emphasis he put on it. The exact contrast to this was when I started driving with Emerson Fittipaldi. His English wasn't very good and either the car was wonderful or terrible, and you couldn't tell what he was enthusing or complaining about. With no shades of meaning it is very difficult to communicate and whereas Jimmy and I were talking on a completely different level, me as the engineer

When not driving Jim Clark was always willing to help out in the pits, such as here at Rouen where he held out his own signal telling Trevor Taylor that he had retired.

and him as the driver, we still managed to communicate very well.'

Today, many years later, Jimmy Clark's influence on Colin Chapman can still be seen. 'I find it very difficult to start thinking about Jimmy even to this day. I've never been able to read his first book. I have a copy at my holiday home and I keep trying to read it but have to give up. No one ever before or since will have such a profound effect on me, we got on so well together and I think he represented an ideal that I would like to achieve. I felt his personal integrity and personal mode of life and values were fantastic. As a man he meant more to me than any other man. He was so thoroughly well brought up and so thoroughly well adjusted to life I felt there was so much good in him that it improved me in some ways.'

One love which Jimmy shared with Colin was the love of flying, as Jimmy was a natural pilot. He fitted very easily into the strict regimen of private flying, where you have to be very meticulous in your planning and operation.

He first got the urge to fly after travelling many thousands of miles with Colin Chapman and Jack Brabham in their planes and he found that, not only was it fun, but it was more convenient to fly than to drive everywhere, and in typical fashion he decided one day to learn how to fly. Once Jimmy Clark made a decision like that there was no stopping him. He was competing in the Tasman series in Australia at the time, and he took advantage of the good and consistent flying conditions out there to cram in every bit of training and practice that he could. With his usual dedication he literally lived at the flying club, and worked at it until he qualified as a pilot and bought Colin Chapman's single-engined Commanche. He later bought Colin's Twin Commanche and, after winning Indianapolis in 1965, he ordered a brand-new plane from the manufacturers which was fitted with long-range tanks. The plane, however, disappeared on its delivery flight and was never heard of again: rumours still persist that it wasn't lost over the Atlantic, as was

During the last years of his life Jim was an enthusiastic pilot and owned this Piper Twin Commanche which he loved. He used it both in Britain and during his year's exile in France, and it was in this plane that he flew from Paris to Hockenheim for his last race.

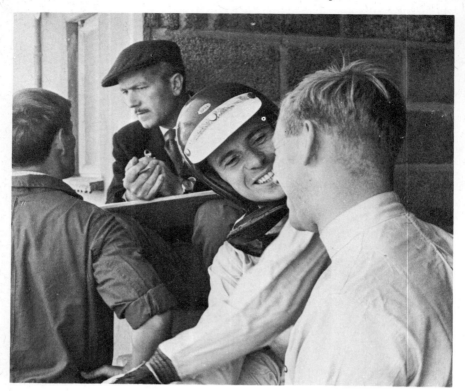

Jimmy Clark and Mike Spence were good friends throughout their racing careers. Both had raced in Formula Junior and Spence joined the Lotus team. In 1968 Clark tested the Lotus Turbine for Indianapolis and then was killed. Tragically, Spence then went to Indianapolis and in practice crashed the Turbine into the wall. Normally this would have given the driver a severe shake-up, but by a quirk of fate the front wheel broke off and hit Spence, killing him instantly. Clark was photographed with Spence, back to the camera, at Brands Hatch.

suspected, but that it was flown to Cuba.

By the time he died light aircraft had become a very important part of his life. He was reputed to have a share in a light aircraft rental business in Australia and there were signs that, when he retired from racing, he would go into the aircraft field.

'I think we would have both gone into the light aircraft industry,' says Colin Chapman. 'I told Jimmy many many times that when he was ready to give up motor racing I would give up motor racing and we would go into something together, and for the first time ever, just two weeks before his accident, he told me that he was actually thinking about the day he would give up motor racing. He had never mentioned it previously.'

It was typical of Jimmy that, when he took up flying, he should seek similar experiences to those he found in motor racing. On one occasion he was invited to meet the number one aerobatic pilot in France, Max Delhomme, and when invited to join Delhomme in a demonstration Jimmy agreed willingly. He had a marvellous time: Delhomme proceeded to do the entire world championship tricks routine, with enough spins, twists and turns to frighten anyone.

Afterwards Jimmy enthused about Delhomme's skill, and his only concession towards his stomach after this remarkable display came at dinner when
he uncharacteristically refused the oysters.

At the end of the day, how does motor racing remember Jim Clark?
Certainly he is respected as one of the greatest drivers in the history of the
sport. It is impossible to compare him out of his era, but within his period of
serious racing — from 1960 to 1968 — he was head and shoulders above
everyone. There are few tests of comparable excellence which one can apply
to drivers, apart from counting up wins which can, of course, be misleading,
as mechanical failures and other circumstances beyond the drivers' control
can produce false figures; but it is not generally known that Firestone
conducted a series of tests in 1966 on behalf of team managers, comparing
various drivers by the amount and type of wear they put on their tyres. Some
drivers wore down their front tyres quicker than the back, and a number of
interesting facts came to light. Though I have not actually seen the report, I
believe that both Jack Brabham and Graham Hill wore out their back tyres
quicker than their front, while Dan Gurney wore out his front tyres quicker
than the back. Some drivers gave asymmetric wear patterns depending on
whether they seemed to enjoy left-hand corners more than right-hand
corners. When Firestone came to study Jimmy's tyres, however, they found
that there was only a 5% difference in the amount of wear between the front
and the rear, which proved a lot about his superb braking technique and his
balance; no one else came near this figure.

To the ordinary man in the street Jimmy was a folk hero. Jimmy's longtime friend and flatmate, Jabby Crombac, tells of arriving at Monza for the
1,000 km race shortly after Clark was killed. An Italian policeman who was
directing traffic outside the gates was a great Clark fan and had more than
5,000 pictures of Jimmy in his home. When he saw Jabby arrive he drew him
into the side of the road and went over to speak to him about Jimmy, with the
tears pouring down his cheeks.

Back home in Scotland, Jim Clark was revered as no other racing driver

*One of Jimmy Clark's friends
was John Milne (right), a
well-known restauranteur in
Glasgow who used to hold private dinner parties for about a
dozen friends. On the left is
Jackie Stewart, at that time
about to start his motor racing
career. Next to him are stock-
broker Nigel Gibb and the
author.*

before or since. Even Jackie Stewart, who has beaten Jimmy's list of Grand Prix victories and has won three World Championships to Jimmy's two, has never achieved the sincere hero worship reserved for Clark, and yet most of Jimmy's fans never even met him.

To the Scots Jimmy was an ideal folk hero in that he maintained his *sangfroid* despite the turmoil going on around him at race meetings, and most of all he was humble when interviewed. It took Jackie Stewart a long time to get out from the the shadow of Jim Clark back home in Scotland, because Jackie at first appeared just a bit too brash and a bit too cocky for the Calvanistic Scots though, of course, they have since learned to love him almost as much as they loved Jim Clark.

The Scots are a soft-hearted and sensitive nation, despite their rough exterior, and typical of the kind of reaction Jimmy Clark received was this poem sent to him by a millworker in Scotland:

'A proven Champion of the World
O'er tricky tracks you've screeched and skirled
Any mony a braw heid you've uncurled
Wi fear and fright.
As room the hairpin bends you whirled
Like Hell gane gyte.'

It may perhaps not be quite up to Burns' standard, but the personal sentiments and respect are patently sincere. Jimmy himself summed up the Scottish attitude towards success thus: 'If you're a Scot you don't push yourself forward. That's the way I was brought up.'

Perhaps Jimmy Clark's influence upon racing is best expressed in an obituary written 160 years before his death; an obituary to John Cavanagh, one of the great English fives players:

'When a person dies who does any one thing better than anyone else in the world which so many others are trying to do well, it leaves a gap in society.'

Appendix One

It is a sign of our times that any expression of religion or religious conviction in relation to a sportsman tends to be suppressed or else allowed to go unrecorded. Just as sentimentality has often been equated with weakness, so any suggestion of religious interest tends to be dismissed, but two of the finest tributes ever paid to Jim Clark have come from Churchmen, both of them former Moderators of the Church of Scotland, the highest office in that Church. From such sources have come feelings which few have expressed so well or more aptly.

The first was the sermon preached by the late Very Reverend John B. Longmuir, TD, DD, at Clark's funeral, and the second the words of the Very Reverend R. Leonard Small, MA, DD, just over a year later. The occasion was the unveiling of a memorial plaque in the chapel of Loretto School at which Clark had been a pupil.

The plaque had been designed and erected in the chapel in Clark's memory and the Reverend Small commenced his dedication address with the following words:

'I dedicate this memorial plaque to the glory of God and in memory of Jim Clark, former pupil of the school, World Champion racing driver, true friend, trusted team-mate, Christian gentleman, a man after God's own heart.'

He then quoted first Corinthians 9, 24-25 'You know (do you not?) that at the sports all the runners run the race, though only one wins the prize. Like them, run to win! But every athlete goes into strict training. They do it to win a fading wreath; we, a wreath that never fades.'

He then spoke from his own heart with the following words which, I feel, make a fitting Epilogue to this book.

'Some three years ago, a member of my congregation, a retired former teacher from Kirkcudbright, happened to meet in Princes Street a former pupil, Innes Ireland. After chatting a little he said: "Mrs Cuthbertson, there are two friends of mine waiting just around Jenners' corner. I'd like you to come and meet them. Mrs Cuthbertson, this is Jackie Stewart. Jim Clark, this is Mrs Cuthbertson an old teacher of mine."

'The whole group talked together, quite easily and happily, and then the lady said, with obvious deep sincerity, "Innes, I wish you hadn't done this."

' "Why on earth not? they're quite a decent couple of chaps!"

' "It's not that, Innes. It's just that I break my heart with fear when I watch you driving, and now I have three of you to break my heart over."

'It was with precisely that quality of agonising personal involvement that hundreds of thousands of us in Scotland and far across the world, heard the news that Jim Clark had been killed, driving in Germany. None of us who were then adult enough really to register this poignancy of personally felt tragedy will ever erase that memory. No memorial would have been needed to keep such remembering alive, and yet it is just this quality of feeling that has produced all the several memorials to Jim Clark, of various sorts and in differing places.

'This particular memorial plaque in his old school is eminently right and proper. It is right, because any school would be both missing an opportunity and failing in its plain duty if it failed to record in some adequate fashion its pride in having helped to produce someone who proved himself to be the best in the world in any sphere of human achievement, especially in this peculiarly demanding one. It is proper because the years spent by Jim Clark at Loretto were the truly formative years of his life. I am well aware that this particular phrase, on the lips of one of my generation, and still more of a member of my particular profession, is bound to make the flesh of any typical modern schoolboy "grue" with disgusted reaction, because it sounds like a typical pious platitude. In this particular case, like many seeming platitudes, it has the virtue of being inescapably true. It was in the years that he spent between the broad farm acres of the Borders and the walls of this school that Jim Clark was laying the foundations of the fine and famous man he was to become.

'I hope and trust that this plaque, for a very long time, will present a challenge to every boy who may read it, to remember and cherish the values that Jim Clark both expressed and personified. He provides a classic example of the man who does things himself. On this particular week-end I would set him in direct contrast to the 134,000 who yesterday afternoon crammed the slopes of Hampden Park for the Scottish Cup Final between Celtic and Rangers. In an age in which more and more boys and young men are condemned to and content with getting their excitement, thrill and satisfaction at second-hand, he stands out as a supreme instance of the participant, the man who does it himself. This does not mean that we should decry the value of the excitement, thrill and outlets for the emotions provided for the Hampden crowd. Without such outlets, setting aside the comparative few who constitute the vandals and lunatic fringe, one wonders how all this energy would be used. As Chairman of the Parole Board for Scotland I am concerned about the increase in crime, most gravely concerned about crimes of seemingly senseless violence, most of them perpetrated by young men of precisely the age group at which Jim Clark was developing into the central activity of his life, his love for motor racing. I am convinced that much of this senseless violence stems from the fact that more and more of our young men are left with too much unexpended energy which, for want of any better outlet, finds expression in such terrifying ways. This is a major and increasing issue of our time, as we look forward to the prospect of shorter and shorter working hours and automation and mechanisation taking most of the sheer physical labour out of daily work. Let the memory of Jim Clark challenge the boys of this school with much better opportunities than many of choosing what they would like to do to search for and find and develop demanding, exciting and even dangerous things they can do for themselves, rather than watching others do them.

'Jim Clark was not only a World Champion Racing Driver, he leaves the memory of a champion of the individual in an increasingly impersonal age, an age in which we are all of us continually pressurised into the mould of the group, slowly but surely, if subtly forced to conform to the dull pattern of the average and the ordinary in the crowd. Jim Clark takes his place with Chichester, Rose and now Knox-Johnston as a challenging reminder of what a man can do on his own.

'Jim Clark would have been the first — indeed he always was the first — to pay tribute to the team-work on which he so completely depended, the combined efforts of makers, designers, engineers and mechanics, but his was a supremely personal achievement. It was made possible, fundamentally, by his complete mastery of himself. He was able to control all that concentrated power of a modern racing car, because he was always in utter control of himself. This is another great issue of our time in a world where more and more mechanical power, constituting an ever-increasing dangerous potential, is being put at man's disposal. What kind of man is to control this degree of power, and for what purposes?

'Jim Clark also personifies, in a unique degree, the acceptance of total responsibility. Think of the decisions he had continually to make, estimates of speed, judgments of distance, the timing of effort, under all sorts of weather and of road conditions, and on a sometimes overcrowded race-track! Think of making such decisions not over a short and concentrated period of supreme effort, but hour after hour, mile after mile, never slackening for one split second his concentration and control! No one, however skilled, could have taken all the relevant data, fed them into a computer, and dictated to him over two-way radio what he had to do. Every one of these decisions, life-and-death decisions quite literally, he had to take for himself. This, too, is a challenge in a world where responsibility is something to be got rid of at all costs and decisions, especially vital ones, are there to be avoided.

'What made Jim Clark not only honoured but beloved, was not his skill, peerless though he frequently proved it to be, but the kind of man he was in himself. He was on top of the world but never but humble, wearing the highest laurels that fame could bestow, and doing it so unassumingly. Whatever any boy may do when he leaves this school, exercising administrative power, managing big business, using tools of a doctor's blessed profession, or anything else, let him remember that whatever you do in life nothing matters half as much as the kind of man you are in yourself.

'That brings me to Jim Clark's faith. All through this service I have been recalling that the last time I was in the chapel of this school was two years ago last November, as Moderator of the General Assembly of the Church of Scotland, to confirm the boys of Loretto who had chosen to take the important step of declaring their allegiance to Jesus Christ and joining the Church of Scotland. I realised then, and I do so still more now, that a boy taking such a step may well be going against the tide of public opinion, even in such a school as this, standing out and being curiously different from the accepted pattern of thinking and believing or, could it be questioning and unbelief? It interests me that Jim Clark did not choose to be confirmed when he was at school. He waited till he was older. Was it because he felt this step was too important to be taken in any sense automatically, that you had to wait until you felt you were ready, even if that meant waiting some years longer? We have the tribute of the present Moderator, Dr Longmuir, to Jim Clark's unmistakable sincerity when he was preparing for his first Communion in his own parish church. We have it on Dr Longmuir's authority that however far Jim Clark might travel in pursuit of his ruling passion for motor-racing, if he was at home at the week-end he was in his place in church. Estimate that part of the man, Jim Clark, however you choose, he provides a challenging reply to the cynical and glib assumption far too cheaply made that to be a professing and practising Christian in this clever and sophisticated world, you need to be something of a moron and a trifle soft. Jim Clark was clearly neither of these, for no one with less than a very fine mind and tremendous courage and strength of character could have achieved what he did.

'To our human understanding for such a man to die so young must seem sheer waste, wanton, senseless, tragedy. But is it, if we believe that anything lies beyond death, and that this life, be it long or short, is only our testing ground for another life still fuller and more satisfying? Is it unrelieved tragedy to die doing what you love doing, and do better than anyone else? Is it only meaningless waste to go out when you are at the top? This, at least, Jim Clark has added to his many other outstanding achievements: dying when he did, and as he did, we shall never remember him at anything less than his splendid best.'

Appendix Two

Any sportsman must finally be judged on his achievements and Jim Clark's were considerable. Only one driver, his friend Jackie Stewart, has eclipsed his record number of Grand Prix wins but Clark's overall performances in all the cars he ever raced are quite outstanding.

Much is said of Clark's devotion to Colin Chapman and Lotus cars, and it is certainly remarkable to consider that, after signing up with Chapman in 1960, he drove only a handful of cars which were not built by Lotus: the Border Reivers Aston Martin DBR1, two of John Ogier's Aston Martin DB4s, a Ford Galaxie at Brands Hatch, a Ford Fairlane in an American stock car race and the Vollstedt-Ford in the Rex Mays 300 at Riverside in California.

Whereas it is difficult to list every single race in which Clark competed, I feel that the following list of races and results is the most complete to appear.

Rather than publish this list in chronological order, however, I feel it is much more interesting to list the races and results by make and model of car. For instance, probably few people realise that Jim Clark raced 23 different types of Lotus from the Lotus 14 (the Elite) to the Lotus 46; or that the model he drove most often was the Lotus 25 Grand Prix car, followed by the Lotus 18 in various forms and the Lotus 33.

Jim Clark's car by car performances

Sunbeam Mk 3 (Clark's own private car)

Date	Circuit	Event	Result
1956			
June 3	Stobs Camp Sprint	Saloons over 2,000 cc	1st
Sept 30	Winfield Sprint	Saloons unlimited	1st
		Modified saloons unlimited	1st
Oct 7	Brunton Beadnell	High-speed trials	6th
1957			
Sept 1	Charterhall	Sports 1,501–2,700 cc	8th

DKW Sonderklasse (Ian Scott Watson's 3-cyl 2-stroke saloon)

1956			
June 16	Crimond	Sports under 1,200 cc	8th
Sept 30	Winfield Sprint	Saloons under 1,200 cc	1st
		Modified saloons under 1,500 cc	1st
Oct 7	Brunton Beadnell	High-speed trials	6th

Date	Circuit	Event	Result
1957			
June 30	Charterhall	Production Cars Handicap	4th

Porsche 1600S (Scott Watson's 1600 Super)

Date	Circuit	Event	Result
1957			
Oct 5	Charterhall	Production Sports Cars (Handicap)	3rd
		Production Touring Cars (Handicap)	2nd
		BMRC Trophy	1st
Oct 6	Winfield Sprint	Modified saloons (unlimited)	1st
		Sports Cars, 1,501–3,000 cc	2nd
1958			
April 5	Full Sutton	Production Sports Cars, unlimited	6th
April 20	Winfield Sprint	Saloons under 2,000 cc	1st
		Sports Cars, unlimited	2nd
April 27	Charterhall	Sports Cars, under 2,000 cc	Ret
		Sports Cars, 1,501–3,000 cc	4th
May 18	Spa-Francorchamps	GT Specials under 2,000 cc	5th
May 24	Full Sutton	Saloon and GT Cars, unlimited	1st
June 8	Stobs Camp Sprint	Sports Cars, under 2,000 cc	1st
June 21	Crimond	Sports Cars, 1,500–3,000 cc	4th
June 28	Rest-and-be-Thankful Hill Climb	Production Sports Cars, 1,501–2,000 cc	1st
July 5	Rest-and-be-Thankful Hill Climb	Sports Cars, 1,501–2,000 cc	1st
July 6	Charterhall	Touring Cars (Handicap)	2nd
		Production Sports Cars (Handicap)	4th
July 12	Full Sutton	Sports Cars under 1,600 cc	1st
July 27	Winfield Sprint	Touring Cars, modified over 1,500 cc	1st
		Sports Cars, 1,501–3,000 cc	1st
Aug 16	Silverstone	Six Hour Relay Race (Handicap)	22nd
Sept 28	Charterhall	Sports Cars, under 1,600 cc	3rd
1959			
April 25	Charterhall	GT Cars, under 1,600 cc	2nd
June 7	Stobs Camp Sprint	GT Cars, under 1,600 cc	1st
		Sports Cars, unlimited	1st and ftd
July 11	Bo'ness Hill Climb	Sports Cars, under 1,600 cc	7th
July 26	Winfield Sprint	GT Cars, 1,000–2,000 cc	2nd

Jaguar D-type (Border Reivers D-type chassis XKD 517)

Date	Circuit	Event	Result
1958			
April 5	Full Sutton	Racing Cars, over 500 cc	1st
		Sports Cars, unlimited	1st
April 27	Charterhall	Racing, Formule Libre	8th
May 18	Spa-Francorchamps	GP de Spa (over 1,500 cc)	8th
May 24	Full Sutton	Sports Cars, unlimited	1st
		Formule Libre	1st

Date	Circuit	Event	Result
June 21	Crimond	Sports Cars, unlimited	1st
		Invitation Handicap	8th
June 29	Charterhall	Formule Libre	1st
		Sports Cars, unlimited	1st
July 6	Charterhall	Racing Cars (Handicap)	1st
		BMRC Trophy (Handicap)	2nd
July 12	Full Sutton	Formule Libre	1st
		Sports Cars, over 1,500 cc	1st
July 27	Winfield Sprint	Sports-Racing Cars, unlimited	1st
Aug 4	Mallory Park	Sports Cars, over 1,500 cc	1st
		Formule Libre Heat	2nd
		Final	7th
Sept 28	Charterhall	Formule Libre	2nd
		Sports Cars, over 1,500 cc	3rd

Triumph TR3 (Clark's own car: Scottish Motor Show car)

1958

June 8	Stobs Camp Sprint	Sports Cars, under 2,000 cc	2nd
June 28	Rest-and-be-Thankful Hill Climb	Production Sports Cars, 1,501–2,000 cc	3rd
July 5	Rest-and-be-Thankful Hill Climb	Sports Cars, 1,501–2,000 cc	2nd

Lotus Elite (Factory prototype and Scott Watson's cars)

1958

Dec 26	Brands Hatch	GT Cars, unlimited	2nd

1959

March 30	Mallory Park	GT Cars, 1,000–1,600 cc	1st
April 11	Oulton Park	Sports Cars, under 1,500 cc	10th
June 20	Le Mans	24-Hour Race: Overall	10th
		Index of Performance	11th
		1,500 cc Class	2nd
July 5	Zandvoort	World Cup Race	Ret
July 11	Bo'ness Hill Climb	Sports Cars, under 1,600 cc	1st
July 26	Winfield Sprint	GT Cars, 1,000–2,000 cc	1st
Aug 2	Mallory Park	GT Cars, up to 1,600 cc	2nd
Aug 29	Brands Hatch	World Cup Race:	
		Heat 1	1st
		Heat 2	2nd
Sept 13	Mallory Park	GT Cars, 1,000–1,600 cc	1st
Sept 26	Oulton Park	GT Cars under 1,600 cc	1st
Sept 27	Charterhall	Sports Cars, under 1,300 cc	5th
		GT Cars, unlimited	1st
Oct 4	Charterhall	GT Cars, unlimited	1st
		Sports Cars, under 1,300 cc	4th
Oct 10	Snetterton	Three Hours Race	1st
Dec 26	Brands Hatch	GT Cars, unlimited	Ret

Date	Circuit	Event	Result
1962			
Feb 11	Daytona	Inter-Continental GT Race, 1,300 cc class	4th

Lister-Jaguar (ex Bruce-Halford, Archie Scott Brown)

1959

Date	Circuit	Event	Result
March 30	Mallory Park	Sports Cars, over 1,200 cc	1st
		Formule Libre:	
		Heat	1st
		Final	1st
April 11	Oulton Park	Sports Cars, over 1,500 cc	8th
April 18	Aintree	Sports Cars, over 1,500 cc	6th
April 25	Charterhall	Sports Cars, over 2,000 cc	1st
		Formule Libre	1st
May 18	Goodwood	Whitsun Trophy (Sports Cars)	Ret
May 30	Rufforth	Sports Cars, unlimited	1st
		Formule Libre	2nd
July 11	Bo'ness Hill Climb	Sports Cars, over 2,000 cc	1st and ftd
July 18	Aintree	Sports Cars, over 2,000 cc	2nd
July 26	Winfield Sprint	Sports Cars, over 1,500 cc	1st
		Formule Libre	1st and ftd
Aug 2	Mallory Park	Formule Libre:	
		Heat	3rd
		Final	4th
		Sports Cars, over 1,200 cc:	
		Heat	2nd
		Final	2nd
Aug 29	Brands Hatch	Sports Cars, over 3,000 cc	1st
Sept 13	Mallory Park	Sports Cars, over 1,200 cc	1st
		Formule Libre:	
		Heat	3rd
		Final	8th
Sept 27	Charterhall	Sports Cars, over 1,500 cc	Ret
Oct 4	Charterhall	Sports Cars, over 1,500 cc	1st
		Formule Libre	1st
		BMRC Trophy Handicap	13th

Tojeiro-Jaguar (Ecurie Ecosse car written off by Masten Gregory)

1959

Date	Circuit	Event	Result
Aug 18	Goodwood	Tourist Trophy	Ret

Gemini (Formula Junior single-seater)

1959

Date	Circuit	Event	Result
Dec 26	Brands Hatch	Formula Junior	Ret

Lotus 18 (first Lotus rear-engined racing car)

1960

Date	Circuit	Event	Result
March 19	Goodwood	Formula Junior	1st

Date	Circuit	Event	Result
April 2	Oulton Park	Formula Junior	1st
April 10	Brussels	Brussels Grand Prix (F2)	Ret
April 16	Goodwood	Formula Junior	1st
April 30	Aintree	Aintree 200 (F2)	Ret
		Formula Junior	Ret
May 14	Silverstone	Formula Junior	1st
May 27	Monaco	Formula Junior	7th
June 5	Zandvoort	Dutch Grand Prix	Ret
June 19	Spa-Francorchamps	Belgian Grand Prix	5th
July 3	Rheims	French Grand Prix	5th
July 16	Silverstone	British Grand Prix	16th
July 24	Solitude	South German Grand Prix (F2)	8th
		Formula Junior	1st
Aug 1	Brands Hatch	Guards Trophy Race (F1)	Ret
		Formula Junior	1st
Aug 14	Oporto	Portuguese Grand Prix	3rd
Aug 19	Goodwood	BARC FJ Championship	2nd
Aug 27	Brands Hatch	Kentish Hundred (F2)	1st
		Formula Junior	2nd
Sept 17	Snetterton	Lombank Trophy (F1)	2nd
		Formula Junior	1st
Sept 24	Oulton Park	Gold Cup Race (F1)	Ret
		Formula Junior:	
		Heat 1	1st
		Heat 2	1st
Sept 25	Charterhall	Formule Libre	Ret
Nov 20	Riverside	United States Grand Prix	16th
Dec 26	Brands Hatch	John Davy Trophy (FJ)	1st

1961

Date	Circuit	Event	Result
Jan 7	Ardmore	New Zealand Grand Prix	7th
Jan 14	Levin	Tasman Race	2nd
Jan 21	Christchurch	Lady Wigram Trophy	Ret
April 3	Pau	Pau Grand Prix	1st
April 8	Brussels	Brussels Grand Prix	Ret
April 22	Aintree	Aintree 200	8th
April 26	Syracuse	Syracuse Grand Prix	6th
May 6	Silverstone	International Trophy (ICF)	8th
July 9	Silverstone	British Empire Trophy (ICF)	5th
Aug 7	Brands Hatch	Guards Trophy (ICF)	2nd
Aug 27	Roskildring	Danish Grand Prix (F1)	Ret

Aston Martin DBR1 (ex-factory car burned out at Goodwood)

1960

Date	Circuit	Event	Result
April 2	Oulton Park	Sports Car Race	3rd
April 16	Goodwood	Sports Car Race	Ret
May 14	Silverstone	Sports Car Race	Ret

Date	Circuit	Event	Result
May 22	Nürburgring	1,000 km	Ret
June 25	Le Mans	24-Hour Race	3rd overall
1961			
May 28	Nürburgring	1,000 km	Ret
June 9	Le Mans	24-Hour Race	Ret
Sept 24	Charterhall	Formule Libre	2nd
		Sports Cars, unlimited	2nd
1962			
May 12	Silverstone	Sports Car Race	3rd

Lotus 21 (Formula 1 car with Climax FPF engine)

1961

Date	Circuit	Event	Result
May 14	Monaco	Monaco Grand Prix	10th
May 21	Zandvoort	Dutch Grand Prix	3rd
June 3	Brands Hatch	Silver City Trophy	2nd
June 17	Spa-Francorchamps	Belgian Grand Prix	12th
July 3	Rheims	French Grand Prix	3rd
July 15	Aintree	British Grand Prix	Ret
July 23	Solitude	South German Grand Prix	7th
Aug 6	Nürburgring	German Grand Prix	4th
Aug 20	Karlskoga	Swedish Grand Prix	Ret
Sept 3	Modena	Modena Grand Prix	4th
Sept 10	Monza	Italian Grand Prix	Ret
Sept 17	Zeltweg	Austrian Grand Prix	4th
Sept 23	Oulton Park	Gold Cup	Ret
Oct 22	Watkins Glen	United States Grand Prix	7th
Dec 9	Kyalami	Rand Grand Prix	1st
Dec 17	Westmead	Natal Grand Prix	1st
Dec 26	East London	South African Grand Prix	1st

1962

Date	Circuit	Event	Result
Jan 1	Cape Town	Cape Grand Prix	2nd
March 12	Sandown	Formule Libre:	
		Heat	2nd
		Final	6th
Aug 26	Ollon-Villars	Hill Climb	3rd in class

Aston Martin DB4 (John Ogier team car)

1961

Date	Circuit	Event	Result
Aug 19	Goodwood	Tourist Trophy	4th
Oct 15	Montlhéry	Paris 1,000 Km	6th

1962

Date	Circuit	Event	Result
Aug 18	Goodwood	Tourist Trophy	Ret
Oct 12	Montlhéry	Paris 1,000 Km	Ret

Date	Circuit	Event	Result

Lotus 24 (F1 car built to take V8 Coventry Climax and BRM engines)

1962

Date	Circuit	Event	Result
April 1	Brussels	Brussels Grand Prix	Ret
April 14	Snetterton	Lombank Trophy	1st
April 23	Pau	Pau Grand Prix	Ret
April 28	Aintree	Aintree 200	1st
May 12	Silverstone	International Trophy	2nd

Lotus 25 (F1 monocoque car)

1962

Date	Circuit	Event	Result
May 20	Zandvoort	Dutch Grand Prix	9th
June 3	Monaco	Monaco Grand Prix	Ret
June 11	Mallory Park	2,000 Guineas	Ret
June 17	Spa-Francorchamps	Belgian Grand Prix	1st
July 1	Rheims	Rheims Grand Prix	Ret
July 8	Rouen	French Grand Prix	Ret
July 15	Solitude	South German Grand Prix	Ret
July 21	Aintree	British Grand Prix	1st
Aug 5	Nürburgring	German Grand Prix	4th
Sept 1	Oulton Park	Gold Cup	1st
Sept 16	Monza	Italian Grand Prix	Ret
Oct 7	Watkins Glen	United States Grand Prix	1st
Nov 4	Mexico City	Mexican Grand Prix	1st
Dec 15	Kyalami	Rand Grand Prix	1st
Dec 22	Westmead	Natal Grand Prix:	
		Heat	Ret
		Final	2nd
Dec 29	East London	South African Grand Prix	Ret

1963

Date	Circuit	Event	Result
March 30	Snetterton	Lombank Trophy	2nd
April 15	Pau	Pau Grand Prix	1st
April 21	Imola	Imola Grand Prix	1st
April 27	Aintree	Aintree 200	3rd
May 11	Silverstone	International Trophy	1st
May 26	Monaco	Monaco Grand Prix	Ret
June 9	Spa-Francorchamps	Belgian Grand Prix	1st
June 23	Zandvoort	Dutch Grand Prix	1st
June 30	Rheims	French Grand Prix	1st
July 20	Silverstone	British Grand Prix	1st
July 28	Solitude	South German Grand Prix	8th
Aug 4	Nürburgring	German Grand Prix	2nd
Aug 11	Karlskoga	Swedish Grand Prix	1st
Sept 1	Zeltweg	Austrian Grand Prix	Ret
Sept 8	Monza	Italian Grand Prix	1st

Date	Circuit	Event	Result
Sept 21	Oulton Park	Gold Cup	1st
Oct 6	Watkins Glen	United States Grand Prix	3rd
Oct 27	Mexico City	Mexican Grand Prix	1st
Dec 14	Kyalami	Rand Grand Prix	Ret
Dec 28	East London	South African Grand Prix	1st

1964

Date	Circuit	Event	Result
March 14	Snetterton	*Daily Mirror* Trophy	Ret
March 30	Goodwood	International Trophy	1st
April 18	Aintree	Aintree 200	Ret
May 2	Silverstone	International Trophy	Ret
May 10	Monaco	Monaco Grand Prix	4th
May 16	Mallory Park	Grovewood Trophy (F2)	1st
May 18	Crystal Palace	London Trophy (F2):	
		Heat	2nd
		Final	10th
May 24	Zandvoort	Dutch Grand Prix	1st
June 14	Spa-Francorchamps	Belgian Grand Prix	1st
June 28	Rouen	French Grand Prix	Ret
July 11	Brands Hatch	British Grand Prix	1st
July 19	Solitude	South German Grand Prix	1st

1965

Date	Circuit	Event	Result
June 27	Clermont Ferrand	French Grand Prix	1st

Lotus 23 (rear-engined sports racing car)

1962

Date	Circuit	Event	Result
May 27	Nürburgring	1,000 Km	Ret
Aug 6	Brands Hatch	Guards Trophy	Ret
Sept 1	Oulton Park	Sports Car Race	2nd
Sept 29	Snetterton	Three Hours Race	1st

1963

Date	Circuit	Event	Result
April 6	Oulton Park	British Empire Trophy	1st
June 1	Mosport	Sports Car Race	3rd in class
June 3	Crystal Palace	Sports Car Race	1st
Sept 21	Oulton Park	Sports Car Race	1st
Sept 28	Snetterton	Three Hours Race	1st
Oct 13	Riverside	Riverside Grand Prix	1st

Lotus 29 (Indianapolis car similar to 25 with Ford V8 4.2 engine)

1963

Date	Circuit	Event	Result
May 30	Indianapolis	500-mile Memorial Stakes	2nd
Aug 18	Milwaukee	Milwaukee 200	1st
Sept 22	Trenton	State Fair Race	Ret

Date	Circuit	Event	Result

Ford Galaxie (racing saloon)

1963

Aug 5	Brands Hatch	Saloon Car Race	1st

Lotus 19 (rear-engined Lotus sports car fitted with various engines)

1963

Oct 20	Laguna Seca	Monterey Grand Prix	Ret

1964

April 11	Oulton Park	Sports Car Race	1st

Lotus Cortina (Lotus-engined Ford Cortina Lotus 28)

1963

Sept 28	Snetterton	Saloon Car Race	1st

1964

March 14	Snetterton	Saloon Car Race	2nd (1st in class)
March 22	Sebring	Saloon Car Race	3rd (1st in class)
March 23	Sebring	12 Hours	21st (2nd in class)
March 30	Goodwood	Saloon Car Race	2nd (1st in class)
April 11	Oulton Park	Saloon Car Race	1st
April 18	Aintree	Saloon Car Race	3rd
May 2	Silverstone	Saloon Car Race	3rd (1st in class)
May 18	Crystal Palace	Saloon Car Race	1st
Aug 3	Brands Hatch	Saloon Car Race	2nd (1st in class)
Sept 19	Oulton Park	Saloon Car Race	1st

1965

March 13	Brands Hatch	Saloon Car Race	Ret
March 26	Sebring	Three Hours Race	1st
April 10	Snetterton	Saloon Car Race	2nd in class
April 19	Goodwood	Saloon Car Race	1st
Aug 30	Brands Hatch	Saloon Car Race	Ret
Sept 18	Oulton Park	Saloon Car Race	2nd

1966

April 8	Snetterton	Saloon Car Race	3rd (1st in class)
April 11	Goodwood	Saloon Car Race	4th (1st in class)
Aug 29	Brands Hatch	Saloon Car Race	1st
Sept 17	Oulton Park	Saloon Car Race	1st

Date	Circuit	Event	Result
Nov 19		RAC Rally	Ret

Lotus 32 (monocoque F2 car)

1964

April 5	Pau	Pau Grand Prix (F2)	1st
April 26	Nürburgring	Eifelrennen (F2)	1st
July 5	Rheims	Rheims Grand Prix (F2)	4th
Aug 3	Brands Hatch	British Eagle Trophy (F2)	1st
Aug 9	Karlskoga	Canon Race (F2)	2nd
Sept 13	Albi	Albi Grand Prix (F2)	Ret
Sept 19	Oulton Park	Gold Cup (F2)	2nd

1965

Jan 10	Ardmore	New Zealand Grand Prix:	
		Heat	1st
		Final	Ret
Jan 16	Levin	Tasman Cup Race:	
		Heat	1st
		Final	1st
		Flying Farewell	1st
Jan 23	Christchurch	Lady Wigram Trophy:	
		Heat	1st
		Final	1st
Jan 30	Invercargill	Teretonga Trophy:	
		Heat	1st
		Final	1st
		Flying Farewell	2nd
Feb 14	Warwick Farm	Tasman Cup	1st
Feb 21	Sandown Park	Tasman Cup	2nd
March 1	Longford	Tasman Cup:	
		Heat	5th
		Final	5th
March 7	Lakeside	Tasman Cup	1st
April 10	Snetterton	Formula 2:	
		Heat 1	2nd
		Heat 2	5th
		Overall	3rd
April 25	Pau	Pau Grand Prix (F2)	1st
June 7	Crystal Palace	London Trophy (F2):	
		Heat 1	1st
		Heat 2	1st
		Overall	1st

Lotus 30 (backbone-chassis rear-engined sports car, V8-engined)

1964

April 18	Aintree	Sports Car Race	2nd
May 2	Silverstone	Sports Car Race	Ret
May 16	Mallory Park	Guards Trophy	1st
Aug 3	Brands Hatch	Guards Trophy	Ret

Date	Circuit	Event	Result
Aug 29	Goodwood	Tourist Trophy	12th
Sept 26	Mosport	Sports Car Race	Ret
Oct 11	Riverside	*Times* Grand Prix	3rd

1965

March 20	Silverstone	Guards Trophy	1st
April 19	Goodwood	Sports Car Race	1st
May 1	Oulton Park	Tourist Trophy	Ret
June 5	Mosport	Sports Car Race	Ret

Lotus Elan (Lotus 26 convertible sports car)

1964

April 11	Oulton Park	GT Race	1st
May 2	Silverstone	GT Race	1st in class

Lotus 34 (Indianapolis car, updated 29)

1964

May 30	Indianapolis	500-mile Memorial Stakes	Ret
Sept 27	Trenton	USAC Race	Ret

Lotus 33 (F1 car, updated version of Lotus 25)

1964

Aug 2	Nürburgring	German Grand Prix	Ret
Aug 16	Enna	Mediterranean Grand Prix	2nd
Aug 23	Zeltweg	Austrian Grand Prix	Ret
Sept 6	Monza	Italian Grand Prix	Ret
Oct 4	Watkins Glen	United States Grand Prix	Ret
Oct 25	Mexico City	Mexican Grand Prix	Ret

1965

Jan 1	East London	South African Grand Prix	1st
March 13	Brands Hatch	Race of Champions:	
		Heat	1st
		Final	Ret
April 4	Syracuse	Syracuse Grand Prix	1st
April 19	Goodwood	International Trophy	1st
June 13	Spa-Francorchamps	Belgian Grand Prix	1st
July 10	Silverstone	British Grand Prix	1st
July 18	Zandvoort	Dutch Grand Prix	1st
Aug 1	Nürburgring	German Grand Prix	1st
Aug 15	Enna	Mediterranean Grand Prix	2nd
Sept 12	Monza	Italian Grand Prix	Ret
Oct 3	Watkins Glen	United States Grand Prix	Ret
Oct 24	Mexico City	Mexican Grand Prix	Ret

1966

May 22	Monaco	Monaco Grand Prix	Ret
June 13	Spa-Francorchamps	Belgian Grand Prix	Ret

Date	Circuit	Event	Result
July 16	Brands Hatch	British Grand Prix	4th
July 24	Zandvoort	Dutch Grand Prix	3rd
Aug 7	Nürburgring	German Grand Prix	Ret
Sept 17	Oulton Park	Gold Cup	3rd

1967

Jan 7	Pukekohe	New Zealand Grand Prix	2nd
Jan 14	Levin	Tasman Cup	1st
Jan 21	Christchurch	Lady Wigram Trophy	1st
Jan 28	Invercargill	Teretonga Trophy	1st
Feb 12	Lakeside	Tasman Cup Race	1st
Feb 19	Warwick Farm	Australian Grand Prix	2nd
Feb 26	Sandown Park	Tasman Cup Race	1st
March 6	Longford	Tasman Cup Race	2nd
May 7	Monaco	Monaco Grand Prix	Ret

Lotus 38 (Indianapolis car, based on Lotus 34)

1965

May 31	Indianapolis	500-mile Memorial Stakes	1st

1966

May 30	Indianapolis	500-mile Memorial Stakes	2nd

1967

May 30-31	Indianapolis	500-mile Memorial Stakes	Ret

Lotus 35 (F2/3 car)

1965

July 3	Rheims	Rheims Grand Prix (F2)	3rd
July 11	Rouen	Rouen GP	1st
Aug 30	Brands Hatch	British Eagle Trophy (F2)	1st
Sept 18	Oulton Park	Gold Cup (F2)	6th
Sept 25	Oulton Park	Albi	1st

1966

April 11	Goodwood	International Trophy (F2)	Ret
April 17	Pau	Pau Grand Prix (F2)	7th

Lotus 40 (large-capacity sports car based on 30)

1965

Aug 30	Brands Hatch	Sports Car Race:	
		Heat 1	8th
		Heat 2	Ret
Oct 31	Riverside	*Times-Mirror* GP	2nd

Lotus 39 (originally F1 car, but became Tasman car and GP car)

1966

Jan 8	Pukekohe	New Zealand Grand Prix	Ret

Date	Circuit	Event	Result
Jan 15	Levin	Gold Leaf Trophy	2nd
Jan 22	Christchurch	Lady Wigram Trophy	Ret
Jan 29	Invercargill	Teretonga Trophy	Ret
Feb 13	Warwick Farm	Tasman Cup Race	1st
Feb 20	Lakeside	Australian Grand Prix	3rd
Feb 27	Sandown Park	Tasman Cup Race	2nd
March 6	Longford	Tasman Cup Race	7th

Lotus 44 (F2 car based on Lotus 35)

1966

April 24	Barcelona	Juan Jover (F2)	Ret
Aug 21	Karlskoga	Formula 2 Race	3rd
Aug 28	Keimola	Formula 2 Race	3rd
Sept 11	Montlhéry	Montlhéry GP (F2)	2nd
Oct 30	Brands Hatch	Motor Show 200 (F2):	
		Heat	3rd
		Final	3rd

Felday 4 (four-wheel-drive sports car)

1966

Aug 29	Brands Hatch	Guards Trophy:	
		Heat 1	1st in class
		Heat 2	Ret

Lotus 43 (F1 monocoque designed for BRM H16 engine)

1966

Sept 4	Monza	Italian Grand Prix	Ret
Oct 2	Watkins Glen	United States Grand Prix	1st
Oct 23	Mexico City	Mexican Grand Prix	Ret

1967

Jan 1	Kyalami	South African GP	Ret (fuel)

Lotus 48 (F2 car with FVA engine)

1967

April 2	Pau	Pau Grand Prix (F2)	4th
April 9	Barcelona	Formula 2 Race	1st
April 23	Nürburgring (South Circuit)	Eifelrennen (F2)	Ret
May 21	Zolder	Formula 2:	
		Heat 1	1st
		Heat 2	4th
		Overall	Ret
June 25	Rheims	Rheims Grand Prix (F2)	Ret
July 9	Rouen	Formula 2 Race	Ret
July 16	Tulln-Langenlebarn	Formula 2 Race	Ret
July 23	Jarama	Formula 2 Race	1st

Date	Circuit	Event	Result
Aug 13	Karlskoga	Formula 2 Race	3rd
Sept 3	Keimola	Formula 2 Race	1st
Sept 5	Hameenlinna	Formula 2 Race	3rd
Sept 24	Albi	Formula 2 Race	3rd

1968

March 31	Barcelona	Formula 2 Race	Ret
April 7	Hockenheim	Hockenheim F2	Accident —killed

Lotus 49 (F1 car with 3-litre Cosworth engine)

1967

June 4	Zandvoort	Dutch Grand Prix	1st
June 18	Spa-Francorchamps	Belgian Grand Prix	6th
July 2	Le Mans	French Grand Prix	Ret
July 15	Silverstone	British Grand Prix	1st
Aug 6	Nürburgring	German Grand Prix	Ret
Aug 27	Mosport	Canadian Grand Prix	Ret
Sept 10	Monza	Italian Grand Prix	3rd
Oct 1	Watkins Glen	United States Grand Prix	1st
Oct 22	Mexico City	Mexican Grand Prix	1st
Nov 12	Jarama	Spanish Grand Prix	1st

1968

Jan 1	Kyalami	South African Grand Prix	1st
Jan 6	Pukekohe	New Zealand Grand Prix	Ret
Jan 13	Levin	Tasman Cup Race	Ret
Jan 20	Christchurch	Lady Wigram Trophy	1st
Jan 28	Invercargill	Teretonga Trophy	2nd
Feb 11	Surfers Paradise	Tasman Cup Race	1st
Feb 18	Warwick Farm	Tasman Cup Race	1st
Feb 25	Sandown Park	Australian Grand Prix	1st
March 4	Longford	Tasman Cup Race	5th

Ford Fairlane (US Stock Car)

1967

Oct 29	Rockingham	Rockingham 500 (stock cars)	Ret

Vollstedt-Ford (single-seater USAC car)

1967

Nov 5	Riverside	Rex Mays 300	Ret

Index

Note Page numbers in italics refer to illustrations

Agajanian, J. C.   62, *68*
Ahrens Kurt, Jnr   79, 80
Aintree   *18*, 28, *31*, 32, 38
Allison, Cliff   16, 28
American GP   *26*, 29, 32, 37, 43, 49, 52, 59
Amon, Chris   *53*, 54, 76, 79
Argentine GP   22, 23
Arlen, Michael   90
Aston Martin   21, 22, *22*, 23, *26*, 27, 34
Audrey, Cyril   71
Austrian GP   39
Autocar   101
Autosport   9, 21

Baekhart, John   *19*
Baghetti, Giancarlo   28
Bandini, Lorenzo   39
Banks, Warwick   113
Barber, Chris   17
Barcelona   75
Belgian GP   9, 14, 23, 39, *40*
Bell, Derek   76, 79
Beltoise, J.-P.   *78*, 79
Berwick & Dist MC   *10*
Bo'ness   *17*, *21*
Border Motor Racing Club   11, *16*
Border Reivers   13, 14, 16, *17*, 18, *19*, 20, 21, 22, 27, 34
Brabham, Jack   28, 36, 44, 48, 58, 60, 119, 121
Bradzil, Josef   90
Brands Hatch   *16*, 17, *20*, *37*, *38*, 42, *44*
Bristow, Chris   24
British GP   18, 23, 28, 32, 35, 39, *44*, 48, 51
BRM   23, 26, 44, 48, 50, *52*, 73, 100
Buckler   10
Burgh of Duns   88

Calder, Alec   100, 103
Calder, Matilda   103

Campbell, William   *86*, 87, 104
Cavenagh, John   122
Chapman, Colin   *16*, 17, 18, 21, 22, 23, 27, 29, 34, *36*, *41*, 42, *49*, 58, *59*, 61, 62, *68*, *69*, 79, *92*, 104, 107
Charterhall   11, *12*, *13*, *15*, 21, 26, 97
Clark, Mrs Helen   105, *105*, 106
Clark, Roger   *45*
Collins, Peter   9, 89
Coombes, John   76
Cooper Cars   24, 28
Cooper, John   23
Cooper, Michael   97
Costin, Mike   *16*, 17, 18, 22
Costin, Frank   18
Cosworth   50
Cottenham, Earl of   90
Courage, Piers   76, *78*
Coventry Climax   16, 27, 28, 31, 43, 60
Crimond   10, 11, 14
Crombac, Jabby   107, 121
Crystal Palace   107
Cuthbertson, Mrs   123

Delhomme, Max   120
Devine, Suzanne   *69*, 70
Dibley, Hugh   *38*, *116*
Dickson, Tom   *15*, 21
DKW   *10*, 11
Duckworth, Keith   *49*, 83
Dunlop   64, *65*
Dutch GP   23, 27, *36*, 48

Eagle   51
Ecosse, Ecurie   13, *13*, 14, 19, *38*, 100, *116*
Elva Courier   23
Endruweit, Jim   *75*, 83

Fairman, Jack   14
Fangio, Juan Manuel   36
Fengler, Harlan   62
Ferrari   27, 28, 76, 88, 101
Firestone   60, *64*, 79, 83
Flockhart, Ron   *19*, 100

Ford   39, 50, 65, *72*
Ford Galaxie   37, *111*
Foyt, A. J.   *66*, 67, 70
French GP   28, 32, 39
Frère, Paul   27
Full Sutton   13

Gagarin, Yuri   96
Gendebien, Olivier   20, 27
German GP   28, 32
Gibb, Nigel   *121*
Ginther, Ritchie   27, 28, 36, 37, 43
Goggomobil   *11*
Gold Leaf Team Lotus   *53*, 55, 56, 74, 76
Goodwood   18, 19, *19, 22, 25*, 111
Gordon, Peter   11
GPDA   114
Grant, Gregor   *70*
Gregory, Masten   19, 20
Gurney, Dan   31, 32, 36, 37, 39, 51, 58, *61, 64, 66*, 107, 121

Habbeger, Walter   80
Halford, Bruce   18
Henderson, Douglas and Isobel   103
Hill, Graham   16, 17, 23, 32, 34, 35, 37, 39, 42, 43, 44, 48, 50, 51, *70*, 71, 89, 121
Hill, Phil   28, 29, 32
Hockenheim   56, *74*, 75-87, 105
Honda   43
Hughes, Peter   10, *48*
Hulme, Denny   48, *50*, 52, 54
Hunt, James   24

Ickx, Jacky   56, 76, 79
Indianapolis 500   37, 41, 42, 49, 54, 56, 58-73, 107, 119
Ingliston   *113*
Ireland, Innes   13, 22, 27, 29, 34, 100, 101, 123
Italian GP   28, 32

Jackson, Eric   *48*
Jaguar D-type   13, 14, 18
Jarama   114
Jenkinson, Denis   16
Johnsgard, Dr Keith   89, 95
Jones, Parnelli   61, 62, 68
Jowitt, Peter   83

Kingman test track   60, 61
Kling, Karl   78
Knepper, Arnie   *67*
Kyalami   32, 74

Lambert, Chris   76, *78*, 79
Lamplough, Robs   81
Le Mans   21, 27, 51
Leston, Les   70
Lister-Jaguar   14, *17*, 18, *18, 19*, 107
Lola-Chevrolet   41
Longmuir, Very Revd J. B.   123
Loretto School   123
Lotus 11   16
Lotus 12   16
Lotus 18   22, *26*, 27
Lotus 21   27
Lotus 23   21, 32, 37
Lotus 24   31
Lotus 25   31, 34, 38, 58
Lotus 19   37, 38
Lotus 29   60
Lotus 30   38, *41*
Lotus 40   *41*
Lotus 48   56, 74, 75
Lotus 49   50, 74
Lotus Cortina   *37*, 38, *42*
Lotus Elan   38
Lotus Elite   *16*, 17, 18, *20*, 21, *21*, 22
Lotus Team   21, 29
Lotus Turbine   55, 56, 70

Maggs, Tony   *29*
Mairesse, Willy   24
Mallory Park   *23*, 107
Mann, Alan   75
Manney, Henry   97
Matra   55, 76
McBain, Jock   13, 16, 22, 23
McIntyre, Bob   20
McLaren, Bruce   32, 35, 36, 37, 39, *41*, 44
Mearns, Jock   *117*
Melia, Brian   *45, 46*
Melville, Pat   11
Mexican GP   *26*, 37
MG Car Club   *9*
Milne, John   *121*
Milwaukee 200   63
Monaco GP   23, 27, 28, 32, 35, 38, 41, 42, 44, 66
Monza   37, 43, 116, 121
Mosley, Max   79
Moss, Stirling   20, 24, 28, *30*, 78, 89, 96, 100
Mott, Stan   97
Murdoch, Geoff   29
Murray, David   14, 16, 19, 20

Naylor, Brian   11
Niven, Douglas   103
Nürburgring   32, *33, 35*, 36, 39, 43, 48

Offenhauser 58, 60
Oliver, Jackie 76, 79
Oulton Park 38, 42, 112

Parkes, Michael 49
Parnell, Reg 22, 27
Parry, Chris 83
Pearce, Isobel 111
Peddie, Donald and Betty 103
Perdisa, Cesare 9
Pescarolo, Henri 78, 79
Pilette, André and Teddy 9
Piper Commanche 76, 119, *119*
Porsche 27, 31
Porsche 1600 10, 11, *12*, 16, 17
Potts, Joe 20
Pratt and Whitney 73

RAC Rally *45, 46*
Redman, Brian 79
Rees, Alan 76
Reggazoni, Clay 76
Reid, Major R. Tennant *46*
Repco 44
Rheims 24
Rindt, Jochen 49, 76
Rodriguez, Pedro 50
Rodriguez, Ricardo 28
Rutherford, Johnny 95

Sachs, Eddie 62
Salvadori, Roy 22, 23, 27
Scarfiotti, Ludovico 49
Scott Brown, Archie 14, 18, 24
Scott Russell, Peter 88
Scott Watson, Ian 10, 11, *12*, 13, 16, 17,
    88, 97, 98, 102
Shepherd Barron, Richard *20*
Shrimpton, Jean *110*
Silverstone 16, *31, 34*, 35, 51, *93*
Sloniger, Jerry 81
Small, Very Revd Leonard 123
Smith, Ken and Susan 103
Snetterton 60

Somervail, Jimmy 13, 97
Spa 13, 14, 24, 28, 32, *39, 40*, 42, 51
Spence, Mike *120*
Sproat, Stan 20
Stacey, Alan 23
Stanley, Louis *70*
Stewart, Helen 113
Stewart, Jackie *29, 38*, 41, 42, 43, *47*,
    48, 71, 74, 76, 79, 87, 89, 90, 99, 114,
    115, 117, *121*, 122, 123
Stokes, Sally *29, 82*, 107, *108, 109, 110*,
    113, *113*
Stuck, Hans and Hans Joachim 78
Sunbeam Mk 3 9
Surtees, John 23, 28, 36, 37, 41, *41*, 43,
    48
Swart, Eddie 113

Tasman Series 27, 38, *53, 54*, 55, 74,
    119
Taylor, Henry 13, *46, 70*
Taylor, Michael 24
Taylor, Trevor 101, *116*
Tecno 76
Thompson, Mickey 58
Tojeiro Jaguar 13, 19, *19*
Tojeiro, John 19
Tourist Trophy 22
Triumph TR3 *12*
Troberg, Pico 79
Tyrell, Ken 55, 76

UDT Lotus 28, 29, 100, 101

Von Trips, Wolfgang 27, 28, 29

Walker, Rob 100
Warner, Graham *20*
Wayne, Malcolm *23*
Whitmore, Gunilla 111
Whitmore, Sir John 21, 107
Wilkinson, Wilkie 21, 107
Winfield *10*

Zandvoort 23, 31, 32, 35, 42, *50*, 76